The Landis Valley Cookbook

D1709547

Good Eating
to You
Tom Martin

The Landis Valley Cookbook

*Pennsylvania German
Foods & Traditions*

SECOND EDITION

STACKPOLE
BOOKS

LANDIS VALLEY ASSOCIATES

Published by
STACKPOLE BOOKS
5067 Ritter Road
Mechanicsburg, PA 17055
www.stackpolebooks.com

LANDIS VALLEY ASSOCIATES
Landis Valley Museum
2451 Kissel Hill Road
Lancaster, PA 17601
www.landisvalleymuseum.org

Printed in China

10 9 8 7 6 5 4 3 2 1

Photographs by Craig A. Benner unless otherwise noted
Cover design by Caroline M. Stover

Library of Congress Cataloging-in-Publication Data

The Landis Valley cookbook : Pennsylvania German foods & traditions / Landis Valley Associates. — 2nd ed.
      p.   cm.
    Includes bibliographical references and index.
    ISBN 978-0-8117-0467-0 (hardcover : alk. paper)
    1. Cookery, German. 2. Mennonite cookery. 3. Cookery—Pennsylvania—Landis Valley. 4. Pennsylvania Dutch—Social life and customs. I. Landis Valley Associates.
TX721.L3387   2009
641.5943—dc22
                             2008027333

To the memories of George D. Landis and Henry K. Landis,
founders of Landis Valley Museum,
who have helped us gain an understanding and
appreciation of the Pennsylvania German culture.
Their lifelong efforts to preserve all things related to
that heritage have inspired us to share our collective
knowledge of Pennsylvania German cooking and
the folklore and beliefs associated with it.

Contents

This symbol is used throughout the cookbook to indicate recipes given in their original Pennsylvania German form.

Preface

Since the first arrival of German-speaking immigrants to Pennsylvania in 1683, they have been a constant wonderment to the rest of the outside world. These German immigrants became known as the Pennsylvania Dutch. Today, however, many scholars prefer the term Pennsylvania German. In our cookbook, you will find these terms used interchangeably.

The Pennsylvania Dutch are a vast and varied group of people who came from the German-speaking areas of Europe, including parts of modern-day Germany, Switzerland, the Alsace area of France, parts of Poland, and the Slovakian countries. The Pennsylvania Dutch include many denominations, from the "Plain" folks—the Amish and conservative Mennonites—to the more numerous Lutheran and German Reformed. These folks brought with them a rich food history, and by incorporating the foods of the New World into their diet, they created an American regional form of cooking from a true German heritage.

Visitors to Landis Valley Museum have asked us, "Who are the Pennsylvania Dutch? What are their foods, culture, beliefs, and folklore? Where do they come from?" This book attempts to answer many of these questions. The Pennsylvania German heritage is much too complex to fit within the confines of one book. However, we have made an honest attempt to do just so.

We also want to tell you about Landis Valley. Today it's a museum, but until the mid-1900s, it was a small crossroads village. In this cookbook, you will find images of Landis Valley then and now, as well as diary entries by Henry Harrison Landis, father of the museum founders.

The lives of the German-speaking immigrants who came to Pennsylvania revolved around planting, harvesting, and the other seasons of the agricultural year. So, too, does our cookbook. Beginning with April 1, Flittin' (or Moving) Day, and progressing through the year, the book shares with its readers the bounty of the seasons.

Many recipes have been graciously contributed by local Pennsylvania Dutch families associated with the museum. We thank those who were kind enough to share their family food traditions with us.

Many individuals and friends of Landis Valley were involved in the first edition of this cookbook, but it really began with our ancestors. We are grateful to those visionaries who kept diaries and journals to record their thoughts so that we might benefit from their foresight.

We thank all of the original committee members who gathered the original recipes and traditions for the first edition of this cookbook into one beautiful volume. We also thank Craig A. Benner, the primary photographer for this edition, and Michael A. Occhionero, the first-edition photographer. Tom Martin was once again a huge contributor to the additions and corrections to this edition. Thank you to Mike Emery for behind-the-scenes contributions. Recognition also goes to Kaye Peloquin, for completing the duties of museum editor for this edition.

Our hopes and wishes are that you not only find good recipes for good eats, but also gain a better insight into our wonderfully rich Pennsylvania German heritage. Our greatest hope and satisfaction is that we inspire present and future generations to learn from the past.

Kumm esse!
Come eat!

The Landis Family Legacy

I n the late 1800s when many Pennsylvania German families still spurned higher education and chose hands-on practical experience over "book learnin'," Henry Harrison Landis and his wife, Emma Caroline (Diller) Landis, of Landis Valley were an exception. Although they lived in rural Lancaster County, Pennsylvania, a predominantly Pennsylvania German area with typical conservative attitudes about schooling, they chose to send their children to college. The Landises encouraged their three surviving children (their firstborn, Anna Margretta, died in 1867) to seek knowledge through schooling and books, as well as learning practical lessons through life experiences.

Their sons, Henry Kinzer and George Diller Landis, both attended Lehigh University and had careers in engineering or engineering-related

The Landis family (from left): Henry K., George D., Henry H., Emma, and Nettie May. Landis Valley Museum Collection, PHMC

fields. Henry lived in New York City, where he edited several magazines, among them *Mineral Industries* and *Gas Age Record.* His many accomplishments included winning yachting awards, singing in a choir, participating in an orchestra, and being a gymnast. George loved the outdoors. An avid hunter and fisherman, he supported local gun clubs and acquired an extensive collection of unusual firearms, including numerous Pennsylvania long rifles.

Their younger sister, Nettie May, also attended college. However, her battle with consumption (tuberculosis) interrupted her education and caused her death at the age of thirty-four.

The Landis family was solid middle-class farm stock. In addition to the farm, Henry H. operated a stone quarry and dabbled in the grain market. For many years, he kept a daily journal. Excerpts from that journal are included in this cookbook to give you a glimpse of life in Landis Valley.

The Landis brothers launched their career of collecting things in their childhood. They first saved birds' nests and eggs. Soon they were on the path that would lead them through a lifetime of acquiring an extensive collection of objects reflecting their heritage.

In 1935, Henry K. penned a story about kitchens and cooking utensils, which appeared in a Pennsylvania German Society publication in 1939. "Where every utensil was designed for some particular use and made largely in the colonies by home talent," he wrote, "there are a technology to be studied and uses to be investigated. . . . In two more generations these survivors will be gone, and it is evident that permanent records made today will save a lot of searching in the future."

George and Henry K. began a formal museum in the 1920s. Their endeavor was expanded in 1940–41 with the help of the Oberlander Trust, Carl Schurz Memorial Foundation, Inc. In a story about the Landis brothers in *The German-American Review* in 1941, Henry K. is quoted as saying: "The future is often influenced by the past. By studying the relics of the past, one better understands the tendencies of the present. It is with these ideas in mind that we should view the Landis Valley collection. . . . Here we find tools, artifacts, implements, vehicles, things actually made and used by the early inhabitants."

In 1953, the brothers presented their immense collection to the Commonwealth of Pennsylvania. This eclectic collection, ranging from books to plows to textiles, is the largest existing body of Pennsylvania German artifacts in the world today. That is the legacy of the Landis family of Landis Valley.

CHAPTER 1

Moving Day
Flittin' and Fressin'

"When a man and his family moved from one farm to another or to a town to retire, it was called a 'Flittin'.' Farmers came with their large four-horse wagons to haul the stuff, their wives and grown children too; the smaller children were usually still at school. Pies aplenty, cakes likewise were baked; victuals of all kinds were prepared, usually plenty of chicken and cold ham. A large spring wagon was loaded with the cook stove and pipe and the eats to be sent ahead to get ready and prepare for dinner."

BIRDES A. JACOBS, 1952

The family cook stove was the first thing to be set up on the day of a flittin'. *Photo by Michael A. Occhionero*

Landis Valley Museum Collection, PHMC

*"This is the business day.
Mama says it is the time for
papers. She and George went
to Lancaster this afternoon.
. . . mama brought me a bottle
of olives, no one liked them so
I had to eat them all myself."*

NETTIE MAY LANDIS DIARY,
APRIL 1, 1896

A pril 1 was the traditional opening of the farm year, so it was a logical time for renters to move to new quarters and to settle debts—a "business day." Moving to a new home required many hands. Dubbed Flittin' Day (Moving Day), April 1 was when friends and family came with their wagons to help move household furniture, farm tools, and other personal effects, as well as help drive any animals to the new residence. The first wagon always held the cookstove, so that it could be reassembled quickly. The women soon had it fired up to do the cooking and baking necessary to feed all those who came to help (fressin' means eating a lot). People often relied upon soup for meals. By augmenting it with bread, pickles, and pies made beforehand, cooks provided a hearty meal for the workers.

"So much money changes hands in Lancaster, on the first, that pickpockets are attracted thither, and the unsuspicious 'Dutch' farmer sometimes finds himself a loser," wrote Phebe Earle Gibbons in *Pennsylvania Dutch and Other Essays* in 1872.

Sometimes this was the day newlyweds moved into their first home as a married couple. Many marriages took place in the fall or early winter after the main farm work was completed, but the couples didn't necessarily live together until later. They might spend their first weeks after the ceremony visiting with various relatives. If the visits ended before April 1, the newlyweds would separate and return to their parents' homes until they could secure their own lodging together.

Ham and Bean Soup

2 ham hocks or a small
    ham end
1 stalk celery
1 pound white marrowfat
    beans
1/2 teaspoon thyme
1 teaspoon parsley
2 small potatoes
1 carrot
1 or 2 small onions
1/2 teaspoon basil
salt and pepper to taste

Soak beans several hours or overnight. Place the ham or ham hocks in a large kettle and cover with water. Cook about 1 hour, and then add the beans and the water they were soaked in. Cook about half an hour, and then add finely chopped carrot, celery, and onions to the soup. Cook until beans are almost too soft, and then add finely diced potatoes to the soup and cook until the potatoes are soft. Add herbs, salt, and pepper. Serves 6.

Cornmeal Rusk

1 1/2 cups cornmeal
1/2 cup dark molasses
1 1/2 teaspoons saleratus
    (baking soda)
1 cup wheat flour
1/2 cup buttermilk

Mix flour and cornmeal together. Add molasses and baking soda. Mix in the buttermilk. Bake in a greased 9-inch cake pan. Bake at 375 degrees for about 15 to 20 minutes.

Keystone Agricultural Almanac, *1842, Philadelphia*

Chicken Corn Soup

**4 to 5 pounds stewing
chicken**

pinch of saffron

1 stalk celery

2 small onions

**6 ears fresh corn on
the cob**

**1 tablespoon finely
chopped parsley**

salt and pepper to taste

noodles (see recipe below)

Wash the chicken well and remove excess fat. Place in a large kettle and cover completely with water. Add some salt and the pinch of saffron. Boil for about 1 to $1/2$ hours, until the chicken is soft. While the chicken is boiling, prepare the noodle dough, finely chop the celery and onions, and cut the corn off the cobs. Remove the chicken from the broth and let cool. Remove the skin and discard. Cut the chicken into small pieces and set aside. Add the cut-up vegetables to the boiling broth. Allow vegetables to boil about 10 minutes, and then add the noodles to the boiling broth. Boil about 20 to 30 minutes. (It may be necessary to add more water as the soup is cooking.) Add pepper, cut-up chicken, and parsley. Serves 6.

Noodle making at Landis Valley Museum.

Noodles

2 cups flour
3 eggs
dash of salt
half an eggshell
    full of water

Add salt to the flour, and then make a well in the center of the flour. Add well-beaten eggs and stir into a dough. Add only enough water to make workable stiff dough. Knead a few minutes, and then turn onto a board and cover with a bowl for 10 to 15 minutes. This makes it easier to roll out the dough. Divide into 3 pieces and roll each piece as thin as possible, sprinkling with as little flour as possible. Lay the rounds of dough on a cloth and let sit about 30 minutes. Turn the pieces over and let dry another 30 minutes. Roll up the dough and cut into thin slices the desired width of your noodles. Add to soup, or cook in salt water and serve as a side dish with melted butter.

Philadelphia Cinnamon Buns (Sticky Buns)

2 cups scalded milk

2 packets yeast

$^1/_2$ cup butter

4 to 6 cups flour

2 teaspoons salt

$^1/_2$ cup granulated sugar

3 slightly beaten eggs

brown sugar

cinnamon

syrup (see recipe on
    next page)

Mix scalded milk, salt, sugar, and butter. Add beaten eggs and then the yeast. Add enough flour to make a soft dough. Knead well and place in a greased bowl. Let rise for about 45 minutes. Divide dough in half, and roll out in rectangles about 15 x 9 inches. Brush melted butter on the dough, and sprinkle with brown sugar and cinnamon. Roll up like a jelly roll and cut into $^1/_2$-inch slices. Grease two 9 x 13-inch pans and spread with syrup. If desired, you can sprinkle in some nuts, raisins, or coconut, and then place the buns in the pan. Let rise until doubled in size. Bake at 375 degrees for about 20 minutes. Take from the oven and let sit for a few minutes. Then dump the buns out of the pans onto a cooling rack. Be careful, the syrup may be hot! Serve warm.

A variety of sticky buns.

Syrup for Buns

1 cup light brown sugar
1 tablespoon molasses
$^1/_4$ cup butter
$^1/_4$ cup water

Place all ingredients in a saucepan and bring to a boil. Boil just until the sugar is melted. Pour into greased pans. Let cool before placing in the cinnamon buns.

Horehound Candy

1$^1/_4$ teaspoons pressed
  horehound (leaves)
2 cups sugar
$^1/_3$ cup white corn (karo)
  syrup
1$^1/_4$ cups boiling water
$^1/_8$ teaspoon salt

Pour boiling water over horehound. Let stand 10 minutes. Strain. Add sugar and salt to the water from horehound. Boil to soft crack stage on your candy thermometer. Pour in thin sheet onto well-buttered baking sheet. Mark into squares before candy hardens.

CHAPTER 2

St. Gertrude's Day
Ode to Spring Onions

Four-square garden at Landis Valley Museum.

Drink up! Almost every farm had an orchard, and apple cider was a staple beverage. Coffee also was popular, but it was sometimes too expensive for the thrifty Pennsylvania Dutch. Coffee substitutes such as roasted rye and barley sometimes were used. Or dandelion roots were dug, cleaned, roasted, and ground to make a beverage. Pennsylvania Germans also made meadow tea from spearmint and peppermint. Blue mountain tea, made from sweet or anise-scented goldenrod, was another favorite. Many teas also had medicinal uses.

Pennsylvania Germans frequently referred to almanacs for planting and harvesting information. *Landis Valley Museum Collection, PHMC*

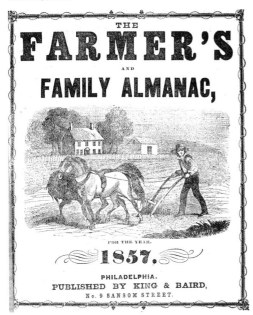

Spring onions are one of the great treats found throughout Pennsylvania Dutch country. The pungent odor of freshly picked onions, with the damp earth still clinging to the bottoms, is pure perfume to the nostrils of a Pennsylvania Dutchman or his Hausfraa (housewife).

Beginning in late April and early May, spring onions are among the first offerings at farm markets and country roadside stands. Farm women put them on the table regardless of other foods being served. Dipped into salt and eaten with thickly buttered bread, these onions transport Dutchmen of all ages into a state of near intoxication. Growing onions is serious business, and woe to any "foreigner" who doesn't understand how it is done!

The process begins with digging the garden. March 17, St. Gertrude's Day (also known as St. Patrick's Day), traditionally is when onions are planted. Three months later, on June 27—the Seven Sleepers—the women and children put the onions to sleep by knocking down their tops. This prevents formation of seed heads. Snug in their warm garden bed, the onions rest throughout most of the summer. On St. James Day, July 25, women and children pull the onions and allow them to dry and cure for several days before putting them into storage for winter use. If they aren't removed by St. James Day, they are likely to rot.

Pennsylvania German cooks use onions in soups, filling or stuffing, and relishes, as well as Zwiwwelboi (onion pie), which is served hot as a main dish.

But it is the spring onions eaten raw that hold a special place in a Dutchman's heart and stomach. After a long winter's diet of dried and pickled foods, the onions are forecasters of the "wonderful good" garden bounty soon to find its way to the table.

Cream Salad Dressing for Lettuce

1 small head of lettuce
1/2 cup sugar
1 cup light cream
2 hard-boiled eggs
1/2 cup apple cider vinegar

Wash lettuce, break up into small pieces, and place in a serving dish. Slice the eggs on top of the lettuce. Mix the sugar and vinegar well, and slowly add the cream to the sugar-vinegar mixture. Pour over the lettuce and serve. Put a little crumbled bacon on top if desired.

"An old German farmer remarked to me to-day that he was very sorry to see that we should have no cherries nor peaches this year—although there is such a profusion of blossoms— because they bloom in the dark of the moon!!!"

JAMES L. MORRIS DIARY, APRIL 25, 1846

Zwiwwelbrot (Onion Bread)

3 or 4 medium onions
2 cups pastry flour
1 teaspoon salt
1 cup buttermilk
3 tablespoons butter
¼ cup lard
1 teaspoon baking soda
assorted fresh or dried
    herbs for topping,
    such as parsley, savory,
    and dill

Peel and finely chop the onions. Fry in the butter until soft but not browned. Set aside; don't drain the onions. Mix the salt and flour; then cut in the lard to make it crumbly. Mix in the baking soda and buttermilk, just until the buttermilk is incorporated. Spread the dough out into two lightly greased 8-inch cake pans. Divide the onions between the two loaves and sprinkle the herbs on top. Bake at 375 degrees until lightly browned, about 20 minutes. (Don't substitute regular flour for pastry flour, which is available at gourmet food stores.)

Landis Valley interpretive staff hard at work at the bake oven.

Minnie-Ha-Ha Cake

1 cup sugar
1 egg
1 1/2 cups flour
2 teaspoons baking
   powder
3 tablespoons butter
1/2 cup sweet milk
1 teaspoon vanilla

Cream butter and sugar. Add egg and beat well. Beat in the vanilla. Sift the flour and baking powder. Add alternately with the milk. Place in one 9-inch greased and floured cake pan. Bake at 350 degrees for about 25 to 30 minutes.

The Standard Cook Book, *1913 ladies and men's Bible classes of Eden Sunday School, Eden, Pennsylvania, contributed by Martha Stoner*

Onion Pie (Zwiwwelboi)

6 large onions
approximately 2 cups milk
2 tablespoons flour
2 hard-boiled eggs
3 tablespoons butter
salt and pepper to taste

Peel onions and slice into fairly large slices. Parboil until nearly soft and tender. Drain the onions; sprinkle with the flour, salt, and pepper. Place in a 9-inch pastry-lined pie dish. Slice hard-boiled eggs on top, dot with butter, and fill up with milk. Put on a top crust and bake at 400 degrees for about 40 minutes.

Winnie Brendle, contributed by Mrs. Henry Brooks.

AUTHENTIC Recipe Cultivation of Mustard

"There is a white seeded sort and a brown seeded. The white mustard is used in salads along with the cress or pepper grass, and is sown and cultivated the same way. The black is that which table mustard is made of. It is sown in rows, two feet apart, early in the spring. The plants ought to be thinned to four or five inches apart. Good tillage between the rows. The seeds will be ripe in July, and the stalks should be cut off, and when quite dry, the seeds threshed out, and put by for use. Why should any man that has a garden, buy mustard? Why should he want the English to send him out, in a bottle, and sell for a quarter of a dollar, less and worse mustard than he can raise in his garden for a penny? The English mustard is, in general, a thing fabricated, and is false as the glazed and pasted goods, sent out by the fraudulent fabricators of Manchester. It is a composition of baked bones reduced to powder, some wheat flour, some coloring, and a drug of some kind that gives the pungent taste. Whoever uses that mustard freely, will find a burning heat in his side after he has swallowed the mustard. Why should any man who has a garden, buy this poisonous stuff? The mustard seed ground in a small mustard mill, is what he ought to use. He will have bran and all; but, we do not object to rye bread on account of its color! Ten pounds of seed will grow on a perch of ground and ten pounds of mustard is more than any man can want in a year. The plants do not occupy the ground more than fourteen weeks, and may be followed by another crop of any plant, and even mustard if you like. This, therefore, is a very useful plant, and ought to be cultivated by every farmer, and every man who has a garden."

Baer's Almanac, *1829, Lancaster, Pennsylvania*

The last snow in spring usually comes after the onions
are planted and is called the onion snow.

To Roast a Chicken on an Open Hearth

Feeding chickens, c. 1900. *Landis Valley Museum Collection, PHMC*

Take a small chicken of about four pounds and wash it well. If desired, stuff the cavity with celery, onions, and carrots. Herbs may also be added to the cavity or placed under the skin. Sew the cavity shut. Never fill the bird with bread stuffing. It is not safe!

Tie the wings to the body with heavy cotton mason's cord or linen kitchen twine. Use another piece of cord to tie the legs together. Tie one or two cords around the entire bird from top to bottom. Make this cord as tight as possible. As the bird roasts, it shrinks, and the ties may fall off if not tight enough. Now take a long piece of cord, at least 2 yards long, maybe longer, depending on the distance from your crane to the hearth. Thread this cord through the cord around the bird, pull the two ends even, and tie it around the top of the crane. Don't tie it too tightly until you have your bird positioned properly above the hearth—to one side of the main fire and about 6 to 8 inches above the hearth floor. Tie the cord so that you can easily remove it from the crane, as you will have to retie the bird later. Your cord will now be a double cord and just one large loop. Give the bird a twist, and it will rotate back and forth by the twisting and untwisting of the cord.

Start roasting the bird bottom side down first, and roast it for about 1 1/2 hours. Then take the bird off the fire, and retie it so that the top is down and the bottom is up. Place back on the crane and roast another 1 to 1 1/2 hours. Use a brisk fire for roasting. The bird should get nicely browned and not burned. The meat is very nice and juicy, not fatty. Any bird can be roasted on an open hearth, but the larger the bird, the more time it will take. Roast a 12- to 14-pound turkey for about 8 hours.

Easter Season
Onion Skins and der Oschderhaas

"Whitsun Monday—
a holiday among the Amish
and other German of our
neighborhood, but altogether
disregarded by the English
part of the community."

James L. Morris Diary,
June 1, 1846

Mr. and Mrs. Michael Emery

Don't sew on Shrove Tuesday, or you sew up the chicken's egg hole and the chicken won't lay eggs.

Christians believe Easter is a season of rebirth and renewal. Farmers feel the same way about springtime. The Pennsylvania Germans, composed largely of Christian farmers, felt the life juices rising in their veins in the spring, just as the sap rises in the maple trees. Easter and springtime meant rebirth, renewal, planting, festivals, and FOOD! Religion fed the soul, but the body insisted on more tangible nourishment. It was a time to celebrate the end of the six weeks of want when preserved food was nearly gone. After a winter diet of dried and pickled foods, people embraced with a passion the first coltsfoot tea and dandelion greens served with bacon dressing.

From Fastnacht Day (Shrove Tuesday) to Whiskeytide (Whitmonday, the day after Whitsunday, which is the seventh Sunday after Easter), the Pennsylvania Germans marked the season with liberal doses of food and festivals, both religious and secular, producing some unusual traditions and folklore.

Fastnacht Day

Fastnacht Day (pronounced faws-nacht) was filled with good-natured fun, teasing, and name calling. Fastnacht Day is the Pennsylvania German name for Shrove Tuesday, the day before Lent begins. The first one out of bed was dubbed the cleaning rag or the gander or such. The last one out of bed was in for a day full of razzing and was called the Fastnacht or the old cluck. He or she was the butt of jokes, both at home and at school.

Fastnachts are a doughnutlike treat made of either raised or unraised dough, depending on the locality in Pennsylvania Dutch country. Traditionally, they were made in the shape of a rectangle with a center slit, and deep-fried in lard.

Bakers made rabbit-shaped bread with a strategically placed egg.

> *"Shrove Tuesday is a festival. The darker the coffee and the molasses, the better the taste of the dunked doughnuts."*
>
> RUSSELL W. GILBERT, MID-1900S PENNSYLVANIA GERMAN POET

Today Fastnacht Day still is observed, but the fastnachts often are made in the more familiar doughnut shape.

Fastnachts were split open and smeared with molasses, and then dunked into saffron or blue balsam tea. Traditionalists insist that true fastnacht kuchen (cakes) are made without yeast, and made only on Shrove Tuesday or the day before and eaten on Shrove Tuesday. Also, they omit molasses and spread the fastnacht with quince jam or crab-apple jelly. A fourth-generation Berks County resident explained this method of eating fastnachts in Alfred L. Shoemaker's *Eastertide in Pennsylvania*.

In Pennsylvania German folklore, the first three fastnachts made were fed to the chickens to keep them safe from chicken hawks. The lard used to fry the delicacy was believed to possess special powers. Some felt it could heal human and animal problems. Many believed that it should be smeared on a cow's udders to heal them, if they were sore. Some said that if you greased

On Maundy Thursday, eat something green for good health.

PENNSYLVANIA GERMAN
FOLKLORE

your shovel with fastnacht lard before digging your garden, it would keep the bugs from your vegetables.

The ultimate prediction threatened those who failed to eat fastnachts on Shrove Tuesday: They would get boils, their chickens wouldn't lay eggs, and their flax crop would fail. Dances were held on Shrove Tuesday to ensure a good flax yield. It was believed that the higher the dancers stepped, the taller the flax would grow.

Ash Wednesday

The last one out of bed on Ash Wednesday was called the eschepuddel (the ash pile). The day was full of teasing. Family and friends relished the practice of rubbing ashes on the eschepuddel's face.

The last one to get to school was rolled in the ash pile and had to carry out the ashes from the school stove. Farmers sprinkled ashes on the livestock on Ash Wednesday to keep them free of lice. Phebe Earle Gibbons wrote in *The Pennsylvania Dutch and Other Essays,* "Seven years ago I witnessed a sale of a large stock of cattle, on Ash Wednesday; every cow and steer offered for sale was completely covered with wood ashes."

Ashes also were scattered on poultry, fruit trees, and the garden to keep away insects and to "take the lice to death."

Maundy Thursday

Maundy Thursday is the Thursday before Easter Sunday. Maundy Thursday was known as Green Thursday to the Pennsylvania Germans, and believers ate something green that day to ensure good health. If they were available, dandelions were the traditional meal. Other acceptable greens included endive, turnip greens, cabbage, alfalfa, clover, or herbs. The weather often determined the menu.

Stove, 1857.
Landis Valley Museum Collection, PHMC

Good Friday

Friday traditionally was bake day, but Pennsylvania German women wouldn't bake on Good Friday, the Friday before Easter—they believed baking that day was like staring into the empty tomb. Neither did they do any but necessary chores, because it was a religious day.

There were exceptions to working on that day. Garden work was forbidden between Good Friday and Easter, because Jesus was buried in the earth those three days, yet some felt that cabbage and clover should be planted on Good Friday instead of Maundy Thursday. Sweeping or cleaning on Good Friday was thought to result in good or bad luck, depending on one's personal beliefs. Some said that sweeping on that day would bring ants to your house. Others held that cleaning the cupboards would keep moths and insects out of the house. Some believed that a woman who baked on Good Friday baked someone into or out of the family, meaning the family would have a birth or a death.

Eggs laid on Good Friday were used to help cure disease or ensure good health. Some kept the eggshells and drank water from them on Easter for this purpose. Such an egg stored where it would not be disturbed was thought to protect the house from being struck by lightning. Some maintained that chicks hatched from Good Friday eggs would be speckled.

Much folklore about the weather also was connected with Good Friday. For example, it was said that the sun will never shine clearly before nine o'clock on that morning.

Easter Day

Onion skin–dyed eggs and the Easter bunny. Egg cheese and baked ham. New Easter outfits and egg trees and egg-eating contests. These are the images of a traditional Pennsylvania German Easter.

For centuries, eggs have symbolized rebirth, fertility, and life. The Pennsylvania Dutch, too, saw the egg as symbolic of rebirth at Easter. Weeks before Easter, the boys in the family would raid the hens' nests and hide their eggs, telling Mom that the hens just weren't laying. On the day before Easter, they would appear triumphantly with their collection of eggs. It was a matter of pride for boys to hide as many eggs as possible before Easter and eat as many as possible on Easter Day.

Spring isn't here until all the Easter eggs have been eaten.

PENNSYLVANIA GERMAN
FOLKLORE

Picking eggs was a game very popular with young boys. Challengers would strike eggs together, and the cracked egg was claimed by the victor. Some of the boys garnered quite a stash of eggs that way, particularly if they had a tough guinea hen egg treated with vinegar or a colored wooden egg. And there was always the boy who cracked a fresh, uncooked egg into his opponent's hand, leaving him with a sticky mess dripping from his fingertips.

Boiling eggs in onion skins (outer peelings) produced colors from yellow-gold to a dark mahogany, depending on how long the eggs remained in the liquid. People often scratched designs on the colored eggs and gave them as gifts nestled in small hand-made cardboard boxes covered with wallpaper, called bandboxes. Some still exist as family heirlooms, with dates from the 1800s

Scratch-decorated Easter eggs.

Wash your face in the dew on May 1, without speaking to anyone, to rid your face of freckles.

PENNSYLVANIA GERMAN
FOLKLORE

and even earlier. Often parents or grandparents scratched the eggs as special gifts for children.

Other natural dyes such as hickory bark and walnut hulls also were used to color eggs. Pasting on bits of cloth or natural materials such as binsegraas pith was another means of decorating eggs. Binsegraas (common meadow rush) is a rush that grows in damp meadows and can be found in Lancaster County and surrounding areas. Sometimes people used candle tallow to draw a design on the eggs before dying. The waxed parts remained white.

Egg birds, oschder-voggel in Pennsylvania Dutch, were made by blowing out eggs and attaching folded paper wings, tails, and beaks. These were hung from the living-room ceiling or on branch "trees." Colored eggs were hung on egg trees by the late 1800s. Some egg trees were made of branches anchored in crocks or other containers and displayed inside the house, or eggs could be hung on trees growing outside.

By the late 1800s, commercial establishments were selling dyed eggs, chocolate Easter animals, candy eggs, and glass eggs. As with many Pennsylvania German festivities, some people objected to the Easter bunny, colored eggs, egg trees, and other trappings as too worldly and detracting from the religious meaning of Easter.

If you were Pennsylvania German, your religious denomination probably determined how you celebrated Easter. Like Christmas, Easter was considered by many in the 1700s and 1800s as too holy for raucous celebrations. For others, however, the festivities, food, and games were important additions to the religious rites.

Of all the religious sects the Pennsylvania German culture, the Moravians still continue a unique tradition on Easter Sunday morning. In Lititz and Bethlehem, Pennsylvania, as well as other Moravian towns in the United States, a trombone choir walks through the streets before dawn, heralding in this sacred day.

For Easter dinner, the Pennsylvania Dutch would bring the first ham of the season out of the attic smokehouse, and it made its debut as the star of the meal, accompanied by side dishes such as noodles, potatoes fried in ham fat, dandelion greens with hot bacon dressing, egg cheese, and mint custard pie.

Ham fresh out of the Dutch oven.

"Ham, eggs, and dandelions were eaten on Easter. Often, the first ham of the season was sliced for Easter dinner. Some, however, had the first ham on Good Friday."

TOM MARTIN, 1999

Easter Rabbit

The Pennsylvania Germans introduced the Easter rabbit to America. It was the Palatine German immigrants, from the southwestern Palatine area of today's Germany, who told the world how the Easter rabbit laid the Easter eggs.

As early as the 1680s in Germantown, Pennsylvania, some children prepared nests for the oschderhaas, the Easter rabbit. Often children would set out their caps or bonnets to receive the rabbit's colored eggs. These nests could be set in the house, barn, yard, or even the saffron bed in the garden.

Bakers made rabbit-shaped bread with an egg strategically placed under the tail to prove the Easter bunny laid eggs.

Easter Monday

Easter Monday too was a religious holiday, when only necessary chores should be done. Regular and military parades were pop-

"This afternoon Henry Baumgardner, Frederick Hensel, Godfried Zahm and I were out fishing with their bay net; we went first up the Harrisburg road to Mr. Landis's dam, there we could not catch any."

MATTHIAS ZAHM DIARY, LANCASTER, PENNSYLVANIA, AUGUST 1, 1848

ular on that day. Parades often included fantasticals, groups of people dressed in various costumes, masquerading as minstrels, women, comics, and other characters.

Ascension Day

Ascension Day, forty days after Easter, was the day Christ ascended into heaven. It always fell on a Thursday. Only essential work was permissible on Ascension Day. It was a holy day, not a holiday.

Sewing and pounding nails were expressly forbidden lest lightning strike. Numerous stories were told of those unfortunates who failed to obey and were struck by lightning.

Ascension Day was also known as Fishing Day, and even today in Lancaster County, young Amish boys often are seen that day on their way to a favorite fishing spot with poles in hand. Since Christ ascended into heaven on this day, it was believed that it was a good day for anything that ascended, such as fish from the water.

Conversely, herbs used to cure diarrhea were gathered on Ascension Day because it wasn't a good day for things that

The Aiken and Umble family fishing on Ascension Day, c. 1912.
Mr. and Mrs. Michael Emery

"All spring housecleaning and whitewashing should be done by Whitsunday."

PENNSYLVANIA DUTCHMAN, 1951

descended. People believed that herbs and teas gathered on this day had special health-related powers. Seven and nine were the most popular numbers of herbs to be collected. One source reported, "On Ascension Day Lizzie gathered nine plants for medicinal purposes, three from the woods; dogwood flowers, elder blossoms, winter greens; three from the field; cinquefoil, catnip, ground ivy; three from the garden; horehound, sage, thyme."

Whitsunday (Pentecost) was a religious day observed on the seventh Sunday after Easter. It marked the ascension of the Holy Ghost. In many Pennsylvania German areas, Whitsunday wasn't a major holiday, but the next day, Whitmonday, was.

Whitsunday seemed, instead, to be a basis for folklore. For example, housewives were supposed to have finished all the spring housecleaning and whitewashing, and have other things cleaned up by this day. And if it rained on Whitsunday, it was believed that it was sure to rain for the next seven Sundays.

Whitmonday also became known as the Dutch Fourth of July, because it was a major festival day from about 1835 until the time of the Civil War. Some said that Whitmonday in Lancaster was the greatest gala day of the year. In 1856, one newspaper reported that "it took an extra train to carry this motley crowd into Lancaster."

Occurring between corn planting and haymaking, Whitmonday was an ideal time to party. Schools and industries closed their doors, but stores remained open to serve those from the country who made the annual trek into town to buy their spring clothing.

On the streets, tables and boxes were loaded with oranges, lemonade, ice cream, and groundnuts (peanuts), which cost five cents a pint. Food abounded and also included bananas, leb cakes or lebkuche (gingerbread), popcorn, and a candy called zuckerstengel (mint sticks). Gingerbread sold for "five cents per square foot." Celebrants could drink ginger beer, soda water,

Nettie May Landis. *Landis Valley Museum Collection, PHMC*

or lemonade. Girls and boys would promenade up and down the streets with an orange in one hand and a mint stick in the other.

"I scream! Ice Cream!" cried a Columbia, Pennsylvania, newspaper headline. But food wasn't the only attraction. Bands paraded through the streets. The holiday featured horse and velocipede races, sales, and picnics. Market Square was filled with rope walkers, balloon ascensions, trained mice and monkeys, stereoscopic views, and farm machinery exhibits. There were even "flying horses," a horse-powered merry-go-round costing five or six cents for a circular ride. Vendors sold shoe blackening, razor powder, and patent medicines. People could see hairless dogs, tailless cats, and a fat woman. By the Civil War time period, photographers were available to preserve celebrants' images in pictures.

Flying Horses and Whiskeytide

How did a religious holiday end up being called Whiskeytide?

Whitmonday was also often called Battalion Day, because this was a day when the volunteer militias met for inspection and training. Many local residents gathered at Lenhartsville or Hamburg, Pennsylvania, to watch military parades and maneuvers.

Many revelers were attracted to the dancing and drinking at the local hotels. By 1887, a Lancaster newspaper dubbed the day Whiskeytide and lamented that "whiskey ruled the day."

In earlier times, June fairs had served a similar purpose. But they had been outlawed by local officials by the 1830s because of fighting and drunkenness. How ironic that the religious-based holiday of Whitmonday should come to the same end. Local newspapers editorialized and called for the end of Whiskeytide. "If this be Whitsuntide, for heaven's sake let it die; if it can't die a natural death, let the people and the press take hold of it and choke it," they said.

And choke it they did. The city fathers sounded the death knell by refusing to license the vendors. With little to see, the revelers ceased to appear, and the holiday limped into oblivion.

Egg Cheese

2 quarts cow's milk
dash of salt
4 eggs
dash of sugar
2 cups buttermilk

Bring the 2 quarts of milk to a boil. Meanwhile, beat eggs, and add buttermilk, salt, and sugar. Pour this mixture into the boiling milk. Boil a few minutes, and then remove from the heat and cover. Let sit for about 10 minutes. The mixture should start to separate. Remove the curds and place them in a round or heart-shaped egg cheese mold. Put on a plate and refrigerate overnight. Next day, shake out of the mold and place on a serving dish. Slice and eat with syrup on bread.

The Pennsylvania Germans made tin heart-shaped molds especially for egg cheese and commonly served this cheese for Easter. If you don't have a mold, place the curds in a cheesecloth bag, and hang it up so that the whey drains out of the cheese.

Fastnachts

2 cups scalded milk
1 cup mashed potatoes
3/4 cup sugar
1 package yeast
1/2 cup lard
2 teaspoons salt
2 well-beaten eggs
1 grated whole nutmeg
approximately 7 cups flour

Add mashed potatoes, sugar, salt, and lard to scalded milk. Let cool until lukewarm. Add eggs and nutmeg. Add yeast and enough flour to make a soft dough. Knead well and place in a greased bowl. Cover with a cloth and let rise about 1 1/2 hours. Roll out about 1/4 inch thick on a floured board. Cut with a doughnut cutter or into squares. Place on a cloth and let rise until doubled in size; then fry in hot fat until lightly browned on both sides. Drain on paper. Serve warm with molasses, syrup, or honey, or sprinkled with sugar. Leftover fastnachts can be made fresh again by placing them in a brown paper bag and warming in a 350-degree oven for about 10 minutes.

Helen's Sugar Cakes

2 cups granulated sugar
1 cup lard
1 teaspoon baking soda
4 cups flour
3 eggs
1 cup sour cream
1 teaspoon cream of tartar
icing (see recipe below)
coconut (optional)

Cream lard and sugar. Beat in eggs. Add sour cream, baking soda, and cream of tartar. Add flour. Drop by teaspoonfuls onto lightly greased baking sheets. Bake at 375 degrees for 8 to 10 minutes. They do not brown much. Place on a cloth to cool. Frost with icing and sprinkle with coconut if desired. After icing dries, pack sugar cakes in tins.

Icing

2 tablespoons soft butter
1 tablespoon vanilla
1 1/2 cups confectioners'
   sugar
1/4 cup milk

Blend butter and sugar. Add vanilla. Add enough milk to make a spreadable icing. Beat until smooth.

Fried Ham

Place a large ham steak in a large iron frying pan, without removing the fat. Cover the ham with about an inch of water. Bring to a boil and simmer about 1/2 an hour, turning often. Allow the natural fat in the ham to render out as it cooks, and let the ham brown nicely. Add more water and cook down some more. Cook the ham about an hour total. Remove from the pan and serve with fried potatoes (see recipe below).

Potatoes Fried in Ham Fat

Peel 12 to 15 small to medium-size potatoes, and boil whole until just soft. After removing the ham from your frying pan, add about ¹/₂ inch of water and 2 tablespoons of butter. Bring to a boil and scrape all the ham fat off the bottom of the pan. Remove the potatoes from the kettle and put into frying pan. Cook until the potatoes are nicely browned and all the water is evaporated, turning frequently so they brown evenly. Dish up and serve.

Dandelion Greens with Hot Bacon Dressing

1 quart fresh dandelion
   greens
2 eggs
¹/₂ cup apple cider vinegar
¹/₄ pound bacon
¹/₂ cup sugar
¹/₂ cup water

Gather greens and wash them. Place in a serving dish. Fry the bacon until crisp. Remove from pan, leaving about 1 tablespoon of grease in the frying pan. Beat the eggs in a small bowl. Add sugar, vinegar, and water. Beat well. Add this mixture to the frying pan, place over the heat, and cook until thickened. Pour the hot dressing immediately over the greens. Crumble the bacon over the top. Serve right away. If you don't like dandelion greens or want to make this out of season, you can substitute a small head of lettuce.

Coconut Cake

1 cup butter
2 cups sugar
3 cups cake flour
4 eggs, separated
1 teaspoon salt
1 cup milk
4 teaspoons baking
    powder
1 1/2 cups finely shredded
    coconut

Cream butter and sugar. Add egg yolks and beat well. Add vanilla. Stir flour with the salt and baking powder. Add dry ingredients to butter mixture alternately with milk. Fold in stiff beaten egg whites, and then fold in the coconut. Place in two greased and floured 9-inch cake pans. Bake at 350 degrees for 25 to 30 minutes. Frost with your favorite icing, and sprinkle with more coconut.

 ## Recept for Making Beer

3 lbs of sugar
1 sponfull of creamaterter
1 Lamen

take the suger and lemon and creamaterer and ould [fold] it all together in a stand then make it louk warm then stur yor yeast in to it if your yeast be new take a quart if not new don't as mutch that to make four galouns of Beer let it skim ten or 12 hours then put it in a tite kege shaking it rite well.

Fannie S. Stamen, 1850

Coconut Cream Eggs

5 pounds confectioners'
    sugar
10 ounces of shortening
dash of salt
1 pound, 13 ounces butter
10 ounces cream cheese
2 pounds fine coconut
vanilla to taste
melted chocolate

Cream butter, shortening, coconut, and cream cheese; then gradually beat in sugar, salt, and vanilla. Add more sugar if necessary. Form into egg shapes, and place on wax-paper-covered cookie sheets. Chill several hours. Then dip in melted chocolate. One half batch makes about 100 eggs.

Wheat Bread

1 tablespoon yeast

$^{1}/_{2}$ cup brown sugar

3 tablespoons lard

approximately 4 cups
   whole wheat flour

2$^{1}/_{2}$ cups warm water

1 tablespoon salt

2 cups white bread flour

*Baking Day at Landis Valley
Museum.*

Mix warm water, sugar, lard, and salt. Dissolve yeast and add white flour. Beat well until smooth. Add enough whole wheat flour to make moderately stiff dough. Knead well until smooth and elastic. Place in a greased bowl, cover with a cloth, and let rise about 2 hours. Punch down and shape into two loaves. Place into two greased bread pans. Let rise until doubled in size. Bake at 375 degrees for 35 to 40 minutes. Bread should sound hollow when tapped with your fingers. Place on a wire cooling rack. If you want a soft crust, immediately brush with butter and cover with a cloth until bread is cool.

Kinklings (Cruellers)

2 large eggs
1 cup granulated sugar
$^{1}/_{2}$ cup lard
6 or 7 cups flour
1 whole nutmeg, grated
1 cup milk
$2^{1}/_{2}$ teaspoons baking
powder
dash of salt
1 teaspoon vanilla

Cream sugar, lard, and eggs. Beat until creamy. Add vanilla and nutmeg. Sift flour, baking powder, and salt together, and add alternately with the milk. Add enough flour to make moderately stiff dough. Roll out into long ropes, and form into knots, pretzels, or any shape desired. Fry in deep fat. Serve warm with sugar sprinkled on them.

Onion Skin-Dyed Easter Eggs

1 quart firmly packed
brown or red onion
skins
2 quarts water
1 dozen eggs
1 tablespoon apple cider
vinegar (optional)

Cover onion skins with water and bring to a boil. Simmer about 20 minutes. Remove onion skins and allow the dye bath to cool a little before adding the eggs. Boil about 20 minutes, until the eggs are hard-boiled. Refrigerate and use like any other dyed Easter egg. You can dye more eggs in the same bath, but each batch will be lighter in color.

Note: The addition of vinegar will alter the color, as will the type of pot used. Iron pots will dye eggs very dark brown; brass pots will give a reddish brown color. Use either brown or red skins, as white onion skins produce no color.

Marbleized Eggs

Wrap the eggs rather haphazardly with some of the wet cooked onion skins. Tie them on with a string or use a rubber band. Place these eggs in the dye bath and cook as above. When you remove the eggs from the dye and take off skins, the shells will have light and dark areas, appearing as if marbleized.

Scratch-Decorated Eggs

When the dyed Easter eggs are cool enough to handle, designs can be scratched on the shells with a sharp needle, pin, or knife point. Pennsylvania Germans made these eggs as gifts for the children, scratching names, animals, or flowers on them. The eggs were stored from year to year in little bandboxes and brought out at Eastertime. Over time, the egg will dry up inside the shell. If you attempt to scratch these eggs, be careful not to puncture them, or they will rot and smell bad.

Egg Custard Pie

$^1/_2$ **cup granulated sugar**
4 eggs
$^1/_2$ **nutmeg, freshly grated**
1 tablespoon flour
2 cups milk

Mix the sugar and flour, and beat in the eggs. Add the milk and beat well. Grate the nutmeg half into a 9-inch pastry-lined pie dish, and pour the egg-milk mixture on top. Bake at 375 degrees for about 45 minutes.

 ## Tea Cake

1 quart flour
1 teaspoon soda
$^1/_2$ **pound chopped raisins or currants**
1 cup sour milk
$^1/_2$ **pound lard**

Roll two inches thick. Bake in a quick oven. Split open. Butter and eat while hot.

Henry H. Landis Ledger, late 1800s

Dandelion Wine

2 quarts dandelion flowers

4 pounds white sugar

2 lemons

2 quarts water

1 pack yeast

Pour 2 quarts boiling water over the flowers and let stand overnight. Strain. Discard flowers and add sugar, yeast, and sliced lemons to liquid. Put into a crock and let stand for about 2 weeks, stirring each day. Strain and put into jugs with fermentation locks or wads of sterile cloth. Let sit undisturbed for 4 months. Siphon the wine into another jug, leaving the dregs in the old jug. Let stand for 2 more months. When clear, it can be used.

Mary Zook Harsh, 1870, contributed by Nelda Sweigart

 # Elderberry Blossom Wine

1 quart elderberry
  blossoms

3 gallons water

1/2 cup lemon juice

9 pounds sugar

3 pounds raisin seedless

1 yeast cake

Pick the blossoms careful from the stems and make quart tight full. Put sugar ad water on the fire until the sugar is dissolved let it boil without stirring for 5 minutes scim Add the blossoms as soon as the blossoms are stirred in take from fire and cool when look [lukewarm] put dissolved yeast ad lemon juice in an earthen jar for 6 days stirring thoroughly 3 times a day the blossoms must be stirred from bottom on the 7 day stran through a cloth add rasin. Put in glass preserve glass cover tightly do not use until January.

Grandmother G. M. Landis recipe, contributed by Phyllis Frankhouser

Buwe Schenkel (Filled Noodles)

Peel about 6 to 8 potatoes, and boil until very soft. Mash the potatoes. Fry about ¹/2 pound of bacon very crisp. Drain and reserve some of the bacon fat. Chop fine 2 small onions and snip up a large bunch of chives. Add to the bacon fat, and cook until onions and chives soften. Season with salt and pepper to taste. Allow to cool. Mix a batch of noodle dough, (refer to chicken corn soup noodle recipe on page 5), roll out on a board, and cut into circles using a biscuit cutter. Place a teaspoon of filling in the center of each noodle. Fold noodle dough over, and seal with a little water or crimp together with the tines of a fork. Let the noodles dry a little before cooking in salted water for 15 to 20 minutes. Drain and serve with brown butter or fry them in butter. Serve immediately.

Ham Roasted in Dutch Oven

Select a small whole ham, such as a shoulder (picnic ham), and trim off excess fat. Also remove the rind (skin), and lay the rind on the bottom of the Dutch oven. Place the ham on the rind in the Dutch oven and add 2 cups of water. Cover with lid, and set the Dutch oven on a bed of embers on the hearth. Put hot embers on the lid. Occasionally add more hot embers, on both top and bottom. Roast for about 3 hours. About ¹/2 hour before the ham is done, place sweet potatoes that have been washed and split in half in the bottom of the Dutch oven. Serve ham on a large platter, surrounded with the sweet potatoes. Alternatively, you can bake in a modern oven at 350 degrees for 3 hours.

Thrifty Dutch cooks used expensive saffron for both flavor and color. When placed on a scale, a coin purchased the amount of saffron that was required to balance it. Photo by Michael A. Occhionero

Saffron Bread

Take 25 cents' worth of saffron (1 teaspoon) and pour over it 3/4 cup boiling water. Cover and let sit overnight. Next morning, peel and boil 1 medium-size potato. Cook until soft and mash, saving the potato water. Strain out the saffron. Measure the saffron water, mashed potato, and potato water, and add enough milk to make 3 quarts and 1 pint of liquid. Add to this 2 cups sugar, 1 cup lard, 1 tablespoon salt, and 3 teaspoons grated nutmeg. Add 8 quarts of flour, or enough to make it easy to handle. Add 1 pound of raisins, 1 pound of currants, 1/2 pound lemon and orange peel, and 1/2 pound of candied citron. Knead well. Put in a large greased bowl and let rise until doubled in size. Shape into about 12 to 15 loaves, and place in greased bread pans. Let rise until doubled in size. Bake at 350 degrees for about 35 to 40 minutes.

Estella Hower Smith, c. 1850, contributed by Paul Smith

Peppermint Egg Custard Pie

$^1/_2$ cup sugar

4 eggs

$^1/_4$ nutmeg, freshly grated

1 tablespoon flour

2 cups milk

3 or 4 large sprigs fresh
    peppermint

Tear mint leaves into small pieces, and place on bottom of a 9-inch pastry-lined pie dish. Grate $^1/_4$ nutmeg on top. Mix the flour and sugar. Beat in the eggs. Add milk and mix well. Pour over top of the mint leaves and nutmeg. Bake at 375 degrees until done, about 35 to 40 minutes.

Planked Fish

whitefish or shad

salt and pepper

cooking oil

1 quart potatoes, cooked
    and mashed

lemon and parsley to
    garnish

Scale the fish. Split it down the back. Clean, wash, and wipe dry. Prepare a plank of oak or hickory, about 1 $^1/_2$ inches thick. The size of the plank depends on the size of the oven, but it must be at least 3 inches wider than the fish. Put it into the oven to heat. Rub the fish all over with oil, salt, and pepper. Lay it skin side down on the plank, and put the plank on the top shelf of the oven. Cook about $^1/_2$ hour, spreading oil over the fish while it is in the oven to keep it moist. Form a border of mashed potatoes around the fish using a pastry bag. Set the plank in the oven until the potatoes are browned, and serve garnished with lemon and parsley.

 **Philadelphia Fish Chowder**

Soak about 8 to 10 hard Trenton crackers in a little water to soften, set aside. Take a half pound of bacon and fry it in the bottom of a large Dutch oven. Drain off excess fat. Have about 6 to 8 large potatoes peeled and sliced in thick slices, set aside. Chop 3 large onions, again set aside. Choose a nice fish and cut it up in chunks (about 2 pounds of fish). Start to layer the things in the Dutch oven. Start with a layer of onions, fish crackers, and potatoes. Finish the top with a few crackers. Add about 1 pint of water and put the lid on the kettle and cook slowly for about 1 to 1 1/2 hours. If desired add a little butter and flour to thicken it after the chowder is cooked. Serve with a little chopped parsley. [Milk in chowder was not popular until about the 1850s.]

Eliza Leslie, 1837

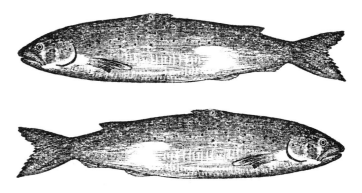

Eel Pie

Cut the eels in lengths of two or three inches, after skinning them; season with pepper and salt, and place in the dish with some bits of butter and a little water, and cover it with paste [pastry]. Middle-sized eels do best.

Brother Jonathan's Almanac, *1863 Philadelphia*

CHAPTER 4

Barn Raisings
They Built It Chust So

Landis Valley Museum Collection, PHMC

"A custom prior to the 1870's or a little later, was to have 'nine o'clock pieces' served in the farm fields. A 'jigger' of whiskey was given as a quencher with fresh water. Boys usually carried some lunch, water and stimulants during the forenoon to hired help, while at work in hay-making and harvest time."

LANCASTER COUNTY HISTORICAL SOCIETY, 1933

A Personal Memory by Tom Martin

We replaced our barn in May 1963. It was a tired, old barn that had outlived its usefulness. The barn was in bad shape when my grandfather bought the abandoned farm in 1933 during the Great Depression. The locals told Grandpa that it might last a few more years if he fixed it up some.

It lasted thirty years.

But time and the elements took their toll, and by 1963, it was time for a new barn. With few exceptions, the method of building Grandpa's barn differed little from barn raisings of the 1800s, and perhaps even earlier.

Preparing and Raising the Barn

Before the day of the raising, many preparations had been made. The masons had laid a new wall, the head carpenter had ordered lumber, and the framework had been laid out. The mortise and tenon joints all were cut and fit together before the barn could be raised. It was like laying out all the pieces of a jigsaw puzzle before you begin to put the pieces together.

The day of construction dawned cool and damp, a typical early spring day in May. The family was up extra early, and I took the day off from school to watch this once-in-a-lifetime event. Before seven o'clock, the first friends and lots of the friendschaft (relatives) arrived. The men assembled into groups ready to build a barn, divided according to their ability to do the various jobs. The older men, who found climbing difficult, would work on tasks such as the flooring, while the younger ones would work on the roof and sides.

One group fetched and placed the floor joist, while another group of men assembled the framework. When all was ready, the head carpenter gave the word, and the men used ropes and poles to pull and push up the frame. The roof rafters were set in place next. The men worked together like a well-oiled machine.

Lancaster County barn raising, c. 1915. Landis Valley Museum Collection, PHMC

"The dishes of smear-case, molasses, apple-butter, etc. are not always supplied with spoons. We dip in our knives, and with the same useful implements convey the food to our mouths."

PHEBE EARLE GIBBONS, 1874

Good Eating

When that many Pennsylvania Germans come together, you can bet your best mule that food was nearby.

When it was time for the nine o'clock piece (coffee break), Katie Beiler, a good friend and neighbor, brought lots of fett kuche (doughnuts). She had been cutting and frying since the wee hours of the morning. And as my granny often said, "Were they ever good!" Since it was a cold day, coffee was also served. Then it was back to work.

As the men worked, the women were busy getting dinner ready. Before I knew it, it was eleven-thirty and dinnertime. (We Dutchmen don't have such fancy things as lunchtime at noon. We have dinner.)

Someone yelled, "Kumm esse" ("Come eat"), and no one needed to be told twice. The men all came filing in with appetites as big as the barn they were building.

Benches were lined up in front of the washhouse with basins, soap, and coarse feed-sack towels for the men to wash up with. Then they sat on long wooden benches at tables while the women served cold sliced ham, potatoes with brown butter, egg noodles swimming in lots of brown butter, and fresh peas.

The Pennsylvania Dutch always started their meal with bread, butter, and a schmiere. A schmiere is something to smear on the bread, like apple butter or jelly. The table also had to have something sour on it, such as pickles or red beets. And no meal was ever complete without a dessert. Usually pies and cakes were served, and sometimes little cakes (cookies) too.

As the men headed back to work, the women sat down to eat and catch up on all the latest gossip. The gabfest didn't last long, because the food had to be put away and all those dishes washed.

A Job Well Done

By late afternoon, the workers headed home to start their evening chores and eat supper. Before the men left, each got a cigar to smoke on the way home as a thank-you gift.

Everyone left exhausted, but with a feeling of satisfaction for a job well done. But the only pay they got was a full stomach. We got a new barn. And I got a memory that will last throughout my lifetime.

Picking the bean harvest at Landis Valley Museum Tavern kitchen garden.

Ham and Green Beans

3 pounds smoked ham
   (2 or 3 large ham hocks
   work well)
2 quarts green beans,
   washed and cut into
   1-inch pieces
$1/4$ teaspoon pepper
6 medium potatoes, pared
   and quartered
vinegar

In a large kettle, cover ham with cold water and simmer 2 to $2^1/2$ hours. Add water while cooking, if necessary, to have at least 1 quart of broth at all times. Remove the ham and cut into bite-size pieces. Add the beans, potatoes, and ham pieces to the broth, and continue cooking for about 25 minutes, until the vegetables are tender. Salt and pepper to taste. Serve with apple cider vinegar.

Egg Dumplings

1 cup milk
$1^1/2$ cups flour
1 egg

Beat egg and milk together, and add flour to make stiff dough the thickness of pound-cake batter. In a kettle, bring 2 quarts of water and a little salt to a rapid boil. Drop the dumplings by tablespoonfuls into the boiling water. Boil about 8 to 10 minutes. Remove with a slotted spoon. Drain and place in a bowl, and cover with browned butter. Serve immediately.

Brown Butter

Melt ¼ pound of butter in a small frying pan. Keep stirring the butter until it turns a nice dark brown color. Pour over dumplings, noodles, or green beans.

Field Hand's Drink

3 heaping teaspoons
   brown sugar
1 quart water
3 teaspoons apple cider
   vinegar
1 teaspoon lemon juice

Mix all together and stir until sugar is dissolved. You may want more lemon juice to give it a lemony taste.

Apricot Preserves

3 pounds fresh apricots
4 cups granulated sugar
3½ cups water

Wash the apricots, cut them open, and remove the pits. Cut apricots into quarters. Place in a pottery or glass baking dish, and put in a 300-degree oven. Roast about 1 hour, stirring occasionally so they do not burn or get too brown. Place sugar in a large kettle and add water. Bring to a boil. Turn down heat and add apricots. Boil gently until the preserves jell. To tell if jelly is done, dip spoon into the mixture, lift out, and turn sideways. If two drops fall off together at one time, it's cooked enough. Place in jars and seal. *Modern-day note:* To keep cooked jams and jellies fresh, place the cooled-down jars in your freezer. The jars will not break if you have allowed enough head space. This keeps the preserves as fresh as when they were first made.

Cracker Pudding

1 quart (4 cups) milk
1 cup sugar
1/2 cup saltine crackers, rolled fine
2 eggs
1/2 cup coconut

Mix all together and cook until the mixture starts to thicken.

Lemon Snaps

1 cup granulated sugar
1/4 cup sweet milk
1/2 teaspoon cream of tartar
2 1/2 cups all-purpose flour
1/2 cup butter
1/4 teaspoon baking soda
juice and rind of 1 lemon

Cream butter and sugar until light and fluffy. Add lemon juice and rind and milk to the mixture. Sift the cream of tartar, baking soda, and flour together, and add to the creamed mixture. Roll the dough out thin on a well-floured board, and cut with a biscuit or cookie cutter. Place on lightly greased cookie sheets. Egg wash the cookies with 1 egg beaten with 1 tablespoon of water, and sprinkle with sugar. Bake at 350 degrees for about 10 minutes, or until lightly browned around the edges. Makes about 1 1/2 dozen 1 1/2-inch-round cookies.

Corn Relish

10 cups fresh corn

5 large onions, ground fine

$^1/_2$ gallon vinegar

4 tablespoons mustard seed

10 cups finely chopped cabbage

3 cups sugar

3 tablespoons salt

1 tablespoon celery seed

Cook everything together for $^1/_2$ hour, pour into hot sterilized jars, and seal.

AUTHENTIC Recipe **Rote Rüben (Red Beets or Rotriewe)**

Red beets are preserved. One boils them and peels off the coarse peel, and cuts them in slices. Then one takes honey or sugar, adds a little wine to it, and boils it. The foam is skimmed off; the syrup is boiled until it thickens somewhat, and then poured over the previously mentioned slices. Then one may season it with the spices which one deems most desirable. It may be kept for daily use. These red beets served as a salad in the winter. One boils peels and slices them as above and then pours over them oil, vinegar, salt and spices.

Christopher Sauer Jr., 1774

Pickled Red Beets

Wash beets and boil until soft. Remove outer skins and cut into slices. Put in a large bowl or crock. Bring to a boil about 2 cups sugar mixed with 1 1/2 cups raspberry-flavored wine vinegar and 1/2 cup water. Cook only until sugar is dissolved. Add salt and pepper. You can add onions, coriander seed, cloves, or horse-radish if desired.

The dialect term *riewe* is applied to turnips, carrots (geel-riewe), tallow turnips, red beets (rotriewe), and red turnips. This is the reason people in Pennsylvania German areas refer to them as red beets rather than just beets.

Pickled Red Beet Eggs

Boil about 2 dozen eggs in lightly salted water about 15 to 20 minutes, until hard-boiled. Cool in cold water, then peel off the shells. Follow the recipe for pickled red beets above, using at least 6 or 8 medium-size beets. Place a few slices of red beets on the bottom of a large glass jar (gallon size). Add eggs, and place several more red beet slices on top. Pour vinegar-and-sugar solution on top, and set aside in the refrigerator for at least 2 days.

Raised Doughnuts

2 packets yeast
3/4 cup water
1/2 cup sugar
1 tablespoon sugar
1 3/4 quarts water
1 quart mashed potatoes
2 tablespoons salt

3 well-beaten eggs
2 cups butter or lard
1 1/2 cups sugar
1 cup scalded milk
about 16 to 18 cups
    of flour

The evening before you want the doughnuts, dissolve the yeast in 3/4 cup water with the tablespoon of sugar. Then add the other ingredients and place in a large bowl. Cover with a cloth and let rise overnight. In the morning, finish preparing the doughnuts as below.

Add sugar, milk, butter, and eggs to the yeast mixture; then add enough flour to make a moderately stiff dough. Knead well. Place in a large bowl and let rise until doubled in size. Roll out dough to about 1/4 inch thickness, and cut with a donut cutter. Let rise until doubled in size, and fry in deep fat. Makes about 160 donuts.

Daisy's Shoofly Pie

Crumbs:
3/4 cup flour
1/8 teaspoon ginger,
    cloves, and nutmeg
1/2 teaspoon cinnamon
1/2 cup brown sugar
dash of salt
2 tablespoons lard

Bottom Part:
1/2 cup molasses
    (King Syrup)
1/2 teaspoon baking soda
1 egg yolk
3/4 cup boiling water

Mix the flour, brown sugar, spices, and salt together, and cut in the lard to make crumbs. Set aside. Mix the baking soda and egg yolk into the molasses. Add the boiling water and stir well. Pour the mixture for the bottom part into a pastry-lined 8-inch pie shell. Sprinkle all the crumbs on top, and bake at 350 degrees for about 30 minutes.

Aunt Daisy, 1930s, contributed by Joan Pyott

Shoofly Pie

Bottom Part:

1 cup molasses
   (King Syrup)
1 egg
1 teaspoon baking soda
³/4 cup boiling water

Top Part:

1 ¹/2 cups flour
¹/4 cup lard
³/4 cup brown sugar

Beat egg and molasses together, and beat in the baking soda. Pour in boiling water and mix well. Set aside. Mix flour and brown sugar, and blend in lard with pastry blender. Take out 1 ¹/2 cups crumbs for top of pie, and add the remaining crumbs to the bottom mixture. Pour this mixture into a 9-inch pastry-lined pie dish. Sprinkle the reserved crumbs on top. Bake at 350 degrees for about 45 minutes. Serve for breakfast.

Vinegar Punch

3 teaspoons apple cider
   vinegar
1 quart water
3 heaping teaspoons
   brown sugar
ginger to taste

Mix all ingredients together and stir well. Put in a jug and take to the field hands.

Harry Stauffer, late 1800s

Funnel Cakes

3 eggs
2 cups milk
3 cups flour
$1/4$ cup sugar
$1/2$ teaspoon salt
2 teaspoons baking soda
deep fat for frying

Beat eggs and add sugar, salt, and milk. Sift flour and baking soda. Add to the egg and milk, and beat until the batter is smooth. It must be thin enough to run through a funnel. If not, add a little more milk. Fill a large cast-iron frying pan about half full of fat, such as lard or Crisco. Heat to 375 degrees. Place your finger over the hole of a household funnel, and fill the funnel half full with batter. Starting in the center of the fat, swirl the batter around the pan until the funnel is empty. Fry until lightly browned, then turn over and fry the other side. Remove from the fat and drain on paper towels. Sift powdered sugar on top immediately and serve. Funnel cakes don't hold well, so serve right away. Recipe makes 25 to 30 cakes. For extra flavor, substitute 1 cup of roasted cornmeal for 1 cup of flour.

Corn Fritters

2 cups fresh grated corn
1 teaspoon baking powder
2 eggs
pinch of pepper
$1/2$ cup flour
1 tablespoon melted
   butter
1 teaspoon salt

Mix grated corn with the salt, pepper, baking powder, and melted butter. Add well-beaten eggs and flour. Mix well, and drop by tablespoonfuls into hot frying pan with a little shortening. Fritters should be the size of small pancakes. When browned on one side, turn over and brown the other. Serve hot with syrup or honey if desired.

Cochineal Cake

1 1/2 cups sugar

whites of 5 eggs

1/2 teaspoon alum

1/2 teaspoon baking soda

1 1/2 cups cake flour

1/2 cup butter

1/2 cup sour cream

1/2 teaspoon cochineal
    (ground with mortar
    and pestle)

1 teaspoon cream of tartar

2 tablespoons boiling
    water

Cream butter and sugar, and add sour cream. Mix the cochineal powder and alum. Pour the boiling water over the mixture and stir well. Let sit until cool. Mix flour with baking soda and cream of tartar, and add to the creamed mixture. Beat egg whites until stiff, and fold into cake batter. Pour 1/3 of the batter into a separate bowl. Sieve the cochineal mixture over this batter and blend together. Then alternate the red and white batters in a well-greased and floured small bundt pan. It may be swirled a little to make it more marbleized. Bake at 350 degrees for about 30 minutes.

Note: This recipe is based on one in Mrs. Herr's handwritten cookbook in the Landis Valley Museum's collection. Our feeling is that this is the forerunner of the modern-day red velvet cake. For those of you who do not know, cochineal is a scalelike insect found on cacti in Mexico. It has been used for centuries as a fabric and food dye. Maraschino cherries and lipstick once were colored with it.

Green Tomato Pickles

Combine 1 peck (8 quarts) green tomatoes with 6 large onions, sliced thin. Sprinkle with 1 cup salt and let stand overnight. Next morning, drain and add 1 quart each vinegar and water. Boil for 15 minutes. Drain again and add 3 cups sugar, 2 quarts vinegar, and 1 teaspoon each cloves, allspice, ginger, mustard, and cinnamon. Boil for 30 minutes, then seal in sterilized jars.

Chow Chow Pickles

1 quart lima beans

1 quart green or yellow
   string beans

4 ears corn

1 pint sweet pickles and
   6 small sour pickles,
   cut up

2 quarts green tomatoes,
   sliced or cut in wedges
   (optional to skin)

1 small bunch celery

1 cup carrots, sliced thin

1 medium head cauliflower

1 quart pickling onions
   (small white)

6 peppers (3 red, 3 green),
   cut in small pieces

Brine

1 cup sugar

$1/2$ teaspoon dry mustard

1 teaspoon cloves

1 teaspoon cinnamon

1 quart combination
   vinegar and the water
   the vegetables were
   cooked in

1 teaspoon mustard seed

1 teaspoon celery seed

1 tablespoon salt

1 teaspoon allspice

If green tomatoes are used, put in brine overnight, using 2 tablespoons salt. In the morning, drain and rinse. Cook all vegetables but the pickles separately, and season to taste. Save the water the vegetables were cooked in, and add the following brine:

Cook over a slow fire until the vegetables are well blended. Add pickles. Mix together 3 tablespoons flour, 1 scant tablespoon of turmeric, and a little water. Add to the other ingredients and cook until the chow chow is smooth, about $1/2$ hour. Seal in sterilized jars. *Note:* These should always be made very early in September.

Pickles (Canned)

6 cups medium-size
    cucumbers

1^1/2 teaspoons salt

1^1/2 cups vinegar

3 or 4 tops of celery

1 onion, cut in 4 pieces

^{1}/2 cup sugar

1^1/2 cups water

5 strips green pepper

Wash pickles, and then jag with fork. Heat pickles in remaining ingredients until they turn color, then put in jars. Seal.

Goldie Heilig Meckley, 1920, contributed by Helen Y. Meckley

Cucumber Cinnamon Rings (Pickles)

Peel and core 2 gallons large cucumbers, and cut in ^{1}/2-inch slices. Dissolve 2 cups of pickling lime in 2 gallons of water, and add cucumbers. Let stand in lime water for 24 hours. Drain well and wash in clear water; then let stand for 1 hour. Drain again. Put in kettle and add 2 cups of white vinegar, 1 tablespoon of powdered alum, and 1^1/2 ounces of red food coloring (a modern addition). Cover and simmer for 2 hours. Drain and set aside while you make syrup.

Syrup

10 cups sugar

2 cups vinegar

8 ounces hot cinnamon
    candies

2 cups water

8 sticks cinnamon

Mix all ingredients together and bring to a boil; then pour boiling syrup over cukes. Each day for the next three days, drain and reheat the syrup; then pour over cucumbers again. On the third day, first pack cucumbers in pint jars; then pour in boiling syrup, and seal.

Chicken Pot Pie

3- to 4-pound chicken
salt and pepper to taste
3 carrots, coarsely cubed
3 or 4 potatoes, peeled
 and quartered
parsley
2 small onions, chopped
pinch of saffron
pot-pie dough (see recipe
 on next page)

Wash the chicken and remove excess fat. Place chicken in a kettle and cover with water. Add salt and saffron, and bring to a boil. Simmer 1 1/2 to 2 hours, until chicken is soft. Remove chicken from the broth and allow to cool. Take the meat off the bones, and cut up into bite-size pieces. Discard bones and skin. Set meat aside. Add carrots, onions, and pepper to the broth. Bring to a boil, and boil for 15 minutes. Add potatoes and boil for 10 more minutes. Roll out pot-pie dough and cut into large squares, about 2 x 2 inches. Be sure the broth is boiling well, and add the dough squares. If there is not enough broth, add more water before boiling the pot pie. Cover and boil for 20 minutes, or until the squares are cooked. Add parsley and chicken and serve.

Chicken pot pie, ready to eat. Kumm esse!

Pot-Pie Dough

1 1/4 cups flour
1 eggshell of water
1 forkful baking powder
(amount a 3-tine fork
will hold without
falling off)
1 egg
1 teaspoon salt

Mix all dry ingredients together, and then add egg and water. Roll out and cut in squares.

Eva Myers, c. 1900, contributed by Martha Xakellis

Coffee without cream and sugar is baarfiessich (barefoot).

PENNSYLVANIA GERMAN FOLKLORE

CHAPTER 5

Baking Day
I Never Met a Pie I Didn't Like

"The baking day was usually Friday; just as washday fell on Monday and weekly clean-up on Saturday or the scouring on Saturday evening."

Henry K. Landis, 1935

> *"If you have four meals a day and a pie at each, many are required. We have a great faith in pie."*
>
> <small>PHEBE EARLE GIBBONS,</small>
> 1874

A Personal Memory by Geraldine Horner

Any way you slice it, bread making in the early to mid-1800s was not easy. Early in the evening prior to baking, Mama went to the cellar to fetch her crock of Satz (homemade yeast) to prepare her bread dough. She filled her dough trough about half full with flour, then added some salt, water, and Satz, mixing and kneading it into a large, springy mass. Then Mama put the lid back on the trough and set the dough near the warm fire to rise.

After waking the next morning well before daybreak to start the day's work, she knocked and shaped the dough into large, round balls, then placed them in linen-lined rye straw baskets, setting them aside to rise again. Meanwhile, the boys got out of bed to get the Briggelhols (bundles of switches used to fire the oven) for her. The girls got up too, to prepare the fruits and custards for the large array of pies. They were taught to roll the dough just right, so that it came out perfectly round, in hopes that they would be ready to find themselves a suitable mate.

After firing the oven for 2 hours or more, Mama could tell if the temperature was just right by the glow of the bricks. She quickly raked out the embers, wiped the oven floor with her Huddelwisch (swab), and tested the oven by sticking her arm in and counting to ten. If she could do so without having to withdraw her arm, it was perfect for her bread. Other women tested the heat of the oven by throwing flour on the oven floor. If it turned light brown, the oven was ready. Black or burning flour meant it was too hot and needed to cool a bit.

When you place a loaf of bread upside down, the angels weep.

PENNSYLVANIA GERMAN
FOLKLORE

Mama needed to work quickly to place the bread in the oven before it cooled. She grabbed the Backoffeschiesser (oven peel), floured it, and dumped the loaves from their baskets. She deftly placed the bread on the oven floor with a quick jerk of the peel, sliding the bread onto the floor for baking. Shutting the door, Mama waited anxiously to see if the bread would be perfectly baked. After the bread was baked, many fruit and custard pies went in. Last of all, she baked a sponge cake or two for Pop or Grandpop. Often these were the menfolk's favorites.

The women and girls spent the time during which the bread and pies were baking by preparing food to be dried. They lined long wooden trays with cloth and arranged slices of fruits and vegetables neatly on these trays for drying in the warm oven. When the baking was done, the oven still retained enough heat for drying. This dried food was used during the winter months; canning didn't become popular in most Pennsylvania German households until after the Civil War. Next morning, the dried foods were bagged in linen sacks for winter storage in the garret (attic).

After all the baking was done, the women and girls scrubbed the tools and utensils, and scraped clean the dough trough, keeping the scrapings for next week's baking. These scrapings were similar to a dried yeast cake. (A good Hausfraa never wasted anything.) The final task for the day was to make a new crock of Satz.

Mama boiled some hops and saved the hops tea. Then she boiled some potatoes, mashed them, and let them cool to lukewarm. She mixed the tea, potatoes, some water, a little sugar, salt, and flour to make a thin batter, and added about a cup of old Satz saved from her previous batch. All this was stirred well and then returned to the cellar to await the next week's baking.

Thus the cycle began again.

Rusks (rolls).

Butter Puff Paste (Pie Dough)

1 1/2 cups pastry flour
6 tablespoons butter
4 tablespoons soft butter
approximately 1/3 cup
  ice water

Mix the flour with the 6 tablespoons of butter, which should be fairly firm. Mix to a coarse crumb, the size of small peas. Add only enough water to make a nice pie dough. It may take a little more or less water. Roll out the dough into a circle, then spread with the 4 tablespoons soft butter. Fold up the dough and roll it out again. Do this three times. Now the dough is ready to roll out and place in a pie dish. Makes one 8-inch pie shell.

Graham Cookies

1/2 pound (1 cup
  plus 2 teaspoons)
  granulated sugar
5 ounces butter
2 cups white flour
1/2 teaspoon vanilla
3 cups graham flour
  (not whole wheat)
1/2 teaspoon salt
1/2 teaspoon baking soda
  dissolved in 1/2 cup
  hot water

Cream butter and sugar. Add other ingredients. Roll thin. Cut into squares with pastry wheel. Bake at 375 degrees for 8 to 10 minutes.

Mrs. Mary Kendig, late 1800s, contributed by Nancy H. Hershey

Pie shells ready for their fillings.

Supper Pies for Baking Day

Since baking day was a long, hard workday, there was little time for cooking supper, so fresh hot vegetable pies often were served as the meal for the evening. Corn pie and potato pie were the two most commonly served vegetable pies. It also was not unusual to sometimes serve hot apple pie or apple dumplings as the supper. These pies were always eaten with hot milk and made a very filling meal.

Corn Pie

6 to 8 ears sweet corn,
 cut off the cob
dash of sugar
butter
2 hard-boiled eggs
salt and pepper to taste
about 2 to 2 1/2 cups milk
pastry for double crust

Line a 9-inch pie dish with pastry. Place about half the corn in the bottom of the dish. Slice one egg on the top of the corn. Add the rest of the corn, and slice the other egg on top. Add the sugar, salt, and pepper. Dot with butter. Roll out a top crust, and cut a hole in the center about the size of a quarter. Place the top crust on the pie, pinch and seal the crust, and cut off the excess dough. Pour the milk in through the hole, filling the pie until the corn is covered. Bake at 400 degrees for about 1 hour. Serve hot with salt, pepper, and milk.

 ## Vinegar Pie

1 egg
1 cup sugar
1 cup cold water
Heaping tablespoon flour
Add 1 tablespoon vinegar
Flavor with nutmeg
Bake with 2 crusts

As it is written, Henry H. Landis Ledger, late 1880s

Potato Pie

6 to 8 potatoes, peeled
  and cut into slices
1 tablespoon flour
1 tablespoon finely
  chopped parsley
  (optional)
2 tablespoons finely
  chopped chives
  (optional)
salt and pepper to taste
2 onions, diced
1 stalk celery, finely diced
1 tablespoon butter
2 to 2½ cups milk
pastry for double crust

Line a large, deep 9-inch pie dish with pastry. Sprinkle flour on bottom of pie shell before adding potatoes. Spread a layer of potatoes on the bottom of the dish, and add some onion, celery, and parsley and chives if desired on top of the potatoes. Keep alternating the layers until the dish is full. Sprinkle salt and pepper on top, and dot with butter. Roll out the top crust, and cut a large hole in the center about the size of a quarter. Place the top crust on the pie, and pinch and seal the two crusts together; trim off excess dough. Pour the milk in through the hole in the top crust, filling the pie until the potato mixture is covered. Bake at 400 degrees for about 1 to 1¼ hours. The potatoes should be soft and most of the milk absorbed into the pie. Serve hot with hot milk over it as a main dish.

Satz (Liquid Yeast)

1 good handful hops
4 to 6 potatoes
3/4 cup sugar
1 teaspoon salt
2 cups water
4 cups water
4 cups whole wheat flour
2 cups of old starter or
    2 packets dry yeast

Add hops to 2 cups of water and simmer for 20 minutes. Then peel potatoes and boil in 4 cups of water. When potatoes are soft, drain and save liquid. Mash potatoes, and add salt and sugar to hot potatoes. Drain the hops, saving the liquid; squeeze the hops to get all the liquid. Add both potato water and hops water to mashed potatoes. Mix in flour, and when lukewarm, add the yeast. Mixture should be like a thin pancake batter. Place in a large crock and let sit overnight at room temperature. Satz is now ready to use. Store in a cool, dark place.

Cream Sponge Cake
AUTHENTIC Recipe

Beat 2 eggs in a cup; fill up the cup with sour cream. Beat in 1 cup granulated sugar, and add the juice and rind of 1 lemon. Mix 1 teaspoon of cream of tartar and 1/2 teaspoon baking soda in 1 cup of all purpose flour. Stir into the mixture. Place in a small greased and floured bundt pan. Bake at 350 degrees for 20 to 25 minutes or until done.

Mrs. Koechling, 1850–90

Coconut Custard Pie

5 eggs
dash salt
1 1/2 cups shredded
    coconut
2 tablespoons butter
3/4 cup sugar
1 teaspoon vanilla
3 cups milk

Beat eggs well; add sugar, salt, and vanilla. Add the milk, set aside. Line a 10-inch pie dish with pastry, sprinkle in the coconut, and dot the coconut with butter. Pour the egg-milk mixture on top of the coconut. Bake at 425 degrees for 15 minutes. Turn the oven to 400 degrees and bake 20 minutes more.

Grape Pie

4 cups Concord grapes
1/4 cup flour
1 teaspoon butter
1 cup granulated sugar
1 tablespoon lemon juice
Crumb topping
   (see recipe below)

Slip the skins off the grapes and set aside. Cook the pulp with 1 tablespoon of water. Simmer for about five minutes, press through a sieve, and discard the seeds. Add the flour and sugar to the pulp and grape skins. Place back on the heat and cook about 5 minutes. Remove from heat, and add the butter and lemon juice. Cool before placing into a pastry-lined 9-inch pie dish. Top with crumb topping, and bake at 400 degrees for about 40 minutes.

Crumb Topping

1 cup flour
2/3 cup butter
1/2 cup sugar
1 teaspoon cinnamon
   or nutmeg, (optional)

Mix flour, sugar, and spice if desired. Mix in the butter to make it crumbly. Spread on top of the pie and bake.

Raisin Bread

about 15 cups flour
3/4 cup warm water
2 cups sugar
1 tablespoon salt
6 eggs
1/3 cup rum
1 cup ground walnuts
3 cups warm milk
4 packets yeast
1 teaspoon sugar
3/4 pound butter
1 cup raisins
1 cup currants
1 cup mixed candied fruit

Mix the water, 1 teaspoon of sugar, and yeast and set aside. Scald the milk and add 2 cups sugar, salt, and butter. Cool until luke-warm. Mix in eggs one at a time. Add the yeast mixture. Blend in enough flour to make a stiff dough. Pour the rum over the mixed fruit, raisins, currants, and nuts, and mix into the dough. Knead well and place in a large greased bowl. Let rise about 2 hours. Punch down the dough and divide into 6 pieces. Shape into loaves and place into greased bread pans. Let rise until doubled in size. Bake at 350 degrees for 30 to 35 minutes.

Contributed by Miss Wilhelmine Barth

Hearty Whole Wheat Bread

5 cups scalded milk

2 tablespoons salt

$1/2$ pound butter

$1/2$ cup caraway seeds

1 cup honey

2 cups rolled oats

3 cups raisins

1 cup wheat germ

1 cup bran

5 packets yeast

8 cups whole wheat flour

6 cups white flour

4 beaten eggs

sesame seeds for on top
   of bread

Mix milk, salt, butter, honey, caraway seeds, raisins, rolled oats, and eggs together. Cool to blood warm. Add the yeast and wheat germ. Add flour and bran until it makes a fairly stiff dough. Knead well. Place in a greased bowl and let rise until doubled in bulk. Punch down and shape into 8 loaves. Place in greased bread pans and let rise until doubled in size. Top with sesame seeds. Bake at 350 degrees for about 35 minutes.

Contributed by Marie Steinmetz

"Went to Lancaster for Bread and Rusks [rolls or buns]. Emma burnt her hand she cannot bake."

HENRY H. LANDIS DIARY, MARCH 25, 1876

Rye Bread

2 packets yeast
$3^1/_2$ cups warm water
$^1/_2$ cup molasses
　(New Orleans)
1 tablespoon salt
2 cups white flour
6 cups rye flour
1 tablespoon lard

Mix the water, molasses, salt, and lard. Add the white flour and beat well. Add yeast. Stir in enough rye flour to make a stiff dough. Knead well. Place in a greased bowl and let rise about 2 hours. Punch down and shape into 2 loaves. Let rise until doubled in size. Slash the tops of the loaves before baking. Bake at 375 degrees for about 45 minutes.

Yeast Raised Waffles

1 teaspoon yeast
2 cups milk
4 eggs
3 or 4 slices stale bread,
　crust removed
1 teaspoon salt
about $2^1/_2$ to 3 cups flour

Tear up bread, add milk, and let soak until soft. Beat up eggs and salt, and then add to the bread-milk mixture. Mix yeast with 2 cups of flour. Beat until about the thickness of pancake batter. Add more flour, if necessary, to make a batter as stiff as pancake batter. Let rise about 1 hour. Then bake in a hot, well-greased waffle iron.

Ten-Egg Sponge Cake

10 eggs, separated
1 pound sugar (2 cups)
$^1/_2$ pound flour ($2^1/_4$ cups)
Juice and rind of 1 lemon

Beat egg yolks until thick and lemon colored. Beat in the sugar and lemon juice and rind. Mix well. Fold in the flour. Last of all, fold in stiffly beaten egg whites. Bake in a large greased and floured bundt pan at 350 degrees for about 45 minutes to 1 hour.

Laura Henrietta (Hensel) Weaver Cookbook, 1870–1900

Molasses Coconut Pie

2 eggs, well beaten
3 tablespoons flour
1 cup coconut
2 cups milk
$^1/_2$ cup brown sugar
pinch of soda
**$^3/_4$ cup molasses
  (King Syrup)**

Mix brown sugar, flour, soda. Add molasses, eggs, and milk. Place the coconut in a 9-inch pastry-lined pie plate. Pour the thick liquid over the coconut, and bake the pie at 400 degrees until the custard is set, about 40 to 45 minutes.

Laura Martin, early 1900s

Walnut Kisses

2 **egg whites**
1 **teaspoon vinegar**
$^{1}/_{2}$ **to** $^{3}/_{4}$ **cup black walnuts**
pinch of salt
$^{3}/_{4}$ **cup granulated sugar**

Beat egg whites fairly stiff. Add salt and vinegar. Gradually add the sugar, and beat until very stiff. Fold in the walnuts, and then drop by teaspoonfuls onto ungreased cookie sheets. Place in a preheated 250-degree oven. Bake 10 minutes. Turn off oven. Leave in the oven for 1 hour, and then remove from cookie sheets. Make about 3 dozen cookies.

Susan Wenger, early 1900s, contributed by Tom Martin

The pies aren't good unless they boil over . . .

Tavern at Landis Valley Museum.

AUTHENTIC Recipe **To Make Pumpkin Yeast**

Cut the Pumpkin into pieces, and put them into a large Bowl with a handful of hops, boil them until the Pumpkin is soft enough to pass through a Cullender, then put it into a large stew Pot, with good yeast to set into fermentation, if well worked & made of a proper Consistence, which must be neither too thick or too thin, it will keep a month or two.

Sarah Yeates Cookbook, 1767–1829

Rosemary Cake

1 cup sugar

1 egg

^{1}/2 cup butter

1 cup sour cream

1 cup all-purpose flour

1^1/2 to 2 teaspoons finely chopped fresh rosemary leaves

^{1}/2 teaspoon baking soda

Cream butter and sugar, add the egg. Beat well. Add sour cream and baking soda. Fold in flour; then fold in the chopped rosemary leaves. Pour into a small greased and floured bundt pan. Bake at 350 degrees for about 25 to 30 minutes.

Grandmother's recipe, late 1800s, contributed by George Roland

THENTIC Recipe Yeast from Potatoes

As is sometimes convenient to know more than one mode of making an article, we have an old method of making potato yeast, which we have somewhere met with. Boil potatoes of the best and most mealy sort, (for poor, heavy, waxy potatoes are good for nothing for this business) till they are thoroughly done and their skins begin to peel off. Strip off the skins, and mash them up very fine, and put as much hot water to them as will make the mash of the consistency of common thick cream. Then add to every pound of potatoes, two ounces of coarse brown sugar, or molasses will answer, and when blood warm, stir in for every pound of potatoes two spoonsful of old or common yeast. Let this ferment for 24 hours. A pound of potatoes will make, in this way, very nearly a quart of yeast and which will keep for three months—so the cook says. She also says you must lay your bread eight hours before you bake it.

Baer's Almanac, *1848, Lancaster, Pennsylvania*

Taylor Cakes

2 eggs
1/2 combination cup butter and lard
1/2 cup buttermilk
3 to 4 cups flour
1 teaspoon cinnamon
1/2 cup sugar
1 cup dark molasses (New Orleans)
1 teaspoon baking soda
1 1/2 teaspoons ground ginger
dash of cloves

Cream butter, lard, and sugar. Add eggs and beat well. Add molasses and spices. Mix in the buttermilk. Add the baking soda and enough flour to make a fairly stiff dough. Refrigerate overnight. Roll out thin on a floured board, and cut with a round cutter. Place on lightly greased cookie sheet. Egg wash the cookies with 1 egg beaten with 1 tablespoon water, and sprinkle with sugar. Bake at 350 degrees for about 10 to 12 minutes. These cookies seemed to be named after Zachary Taylor. There was great interest in the man in the late 1840s, and even a local Lancaster almanac was named for him, *Zachary Taylor's Rough and Ready Almanac.*

How to Make Yeast

Boil 2 good handfuls of hops in a small iron pot for 3 hours, put a plateful of flour in a milk pan, pour the hot water over it while it is boiling, and stir it well all the time with a spoon. Pour more warm water over the hops through the colander until the mixture is like thick paste; then let it stand until it is lukewarm. Add a teacup full of yeast, and stir well. Keep near the stove until evening, when it will be light.

Apple Cake

6 tablespoons butter

2 eggs

1 teaspoon vanilla

1 teaspoon cinnamon

1 cup brown sugar

¹/₂ cup sour cream

1¹/₂ teaspoons baking soda

¹/₄ teaspoon each cloves and nutmeg

2 to 2¹/₄ cups flour

2 cups finely chopped fresh apples

¹/₂ teaspoon allspice

¹/₂ cup nuts or raisins (optional)

Cream butter and sugar. Add eggs and beat well. Add sour cream and vanilla. Sift the baking soda, spices, and flour together. Add to the creamed mixture. The batter will be fairly thick. Fold in the chopped apples, plus nuts or raisins if desired. Place in a small greased and floured bundt pan. Bake at 350 degrees for about 45 minutes or until done.

Never let September winds blow across your hops.

PENNSYLVANIA GERMAN FOLKLORE

Apple Bread

4 apples
2 tablespoons lard
2 packets yeast
1 teaspoon salt
$^1/2$ cup brown sugar
5 to 6 cups flour

Peel, core, and quarter apples. Place in a kettle with about 2 cups of water, bring to a boil, and cook until the apples are tender. Mash the apples well, and then measure the apples plus the water they were cooked in; it should be about 3 cups. If not, add enough water to make 3 cups. Cool to lukewarm. Add sugar, lard, and salt. Add yeast and enough flour to make a moderately stiff dough. (Using half whole wheat flour makes a very nice whole wheat bread.) Knead well and let rise about $1^1/2$ hours. Knock down and shape into loaves of bread or make into rolls. Let rise until doubled in size, and bake at 375 degrees. Bake loaves for about 40 minutes, rolls for about 20 minutes. Rolls can be brushed with melted butter and sprinkled with sugar and cinnamon before baking to bring out the apple flavor. If you want, substitute some unsweetened applesauce and water for the boiled and mashed apples.

Farmer's and Citizen's Almanac, *1839, Philadelphia*

Butter Biscuits

2 cups flour (pastry or
  all-purpose)
$^1/4$ cup sugar
$^1/2$ cup buttermilk
$^1/2$ cup butter
1 teaspoon baking soda

Mix flour and sugar; cut the butter into the flour until crumbly, until it looks like small peas. Mix soda and buttermilk and add to the crumbly mixture. Mix just until incorporated; don't overmix. Roll out about $^1/2$ inch thick on a floured board, and cut with a biscuit cutter. Place on a lightly greased cookie sheet. Bake at 375 degrees for 15 to 20 minutes. Makes about 9 to 12 biscuits.

The aroma of fresh pies out of the oven pleases today's museum visitors.

Montgomery Pie

Top Part:

2^1/$_2$ cups flour

2 cups sugar

2 eggs

3 teaspoons baking
    powder

^{1}/$_2$ cup combination
    butter and lard

1 cup sweet milk

Bottom Part:

1 beaten egg

juice and rind of
    1 lemon

1 cup water

2 teaspoons flour

1 cup sugar

1 cup molasses
    (King Syrup)

Cream shortenings and sugar. Beat in the eggs. Mix the flour and baking powder together, and add alternately with the milk. Set this mixture aside.

For the bottom part, mix the sugar and flour together. Add the lemon juice and rind and well-beaten egg. Add the molasses and water and mix well. Divide the liquid between three 8-inch pastry-lined pie dishes. Spoon the batter on top of the three pies. Bake at 350 degrees for 35 to 40 minutes.

Blueberry or Raspberry Cream Pie

9-inch pastry-lined
   pie dish
1 quart fresh blueberries
   or raspberries
2 tablespoons flour
1 cup granulated sugar
2 cups light cream

Wash the berries and let them drain in a colander. Place the berries in a bowl and add flour and sugar. Toss until well covered, trying not to bruise the fruit too much. Add the cream and stir until well mixed. Place into the pie shell, and bake at 400 degrees for 10 minutes. Then turn the oven to 375 degrees and bake another 30 to 35 minutes. If the pie is not completely set, it will set up more as it cools. Refrigerate and serve cold.

Pie Dough

3 heaping cups pastry
   flour
2 teaspoons salt
scant 1 cup lard
2/3 cup ice water

Mix the flour, salt, and lard until it looks like coarse meal or small peas. Add enough water to make a nice dough. It may take more or less water. Most people tend not to use enough water. Learning to make pie dough is a matter of developing a feel for it. The best way to mix the dough is with your fingers. Makes enough dough for two 9-inch double-crust pies. If using a vegetable shortening like Crisco, use a ratio of 2 cups flour to 1 cup shortening. It is always best to go scant on the shortening.

"These bake ovens were a wonderful institution.
When large numbers of people had to be fed,
as for a barn raising, wedding, funeral,
house-church meeting, etc., the meat in large
chunks was baked in the ovens,
along the rusks, cakes, pies, etc."

HENRY K. LANDIS, 1935

Quilting Bees and More
Fairs, Frolics, and Versammlings

Landis family picnic, c. 1940.
Landis Valley Museum Collection, PHMC

"The extremely popular cakes, twisted, sprinkled with salt, and baked crisp and brown, called pretzels (brezeln) were known in Pennsylvania long before the cry for . . . a glass of lager and two pretzels was heard in the land."

Phebe Earle Gibbons, 1874

Our ancestors had a knack for turning work into a Versammling (gathering, often social). Events such as apple butter boils and corn-husking bees, held in the 1700s and early 1800s, and church quilting bees, held after the 1860s, kept the hands busy while the talking kept the same busy pace. For some, it was hard to do both at once. However, the Pennsylvania Dutch truly believed that "idle hands were the devil's workshop."

Using work as a reason, neighbors assembled to eat, talk, sing, and dance. Games and music gave the young people an opportunity to meet and court the opposite sex. Social gatherings included moving and butchering days, barn raisings, and get-togethers such as cherry festivals and Whitmonday.

At a cherry fair, neighbors flocked to the nearest town or hamlet to visit market stalls filled with fresh cherries, pies, jams, jellies, candy, and other confections. John Hickernell of Schaefferstown in Lebanon County remembers cherry fairs held in the early 1900s in the market building in the town square. Fiddlers wandered through the crowd playing music. And, John noted, the hotels provided ample drinks. Patrons sometimes overimbibed and created ample disagreements. "Oh, they were powerful when they had a few drinks," John said. John's sister was especially fond of dried cherries and bought them to take to school and eat during recess.

A bakehouse. *Landis Valley Museum Collection, PHMC*

Watermelon Cake

Red Part:

4 egg whites
1/2 cup butter
1 cup raisins
2 cups flour
1 cup red sugar
1/2 cup milk
1 teaspoon vanilla
1 teaspoon baking powder

White Part:

2 egg whites
3/4 cup sugar
1/2 cup milk
1 teaspoon vanilla
1/2 cup butter
1 1/2 cups flour
1/2 teaspoon baking powder

For the red part, cream butter, red sugar, and vanilla. Mix baking powder and flour together, and add alternately with milk. Beat egg whites until stiff and fold into batter. Fold in raisins last. *Note:* Use the red sugar sold for decorating cookies, readily available at Christmas.

For the white part, cream butter and sugar, and add vanilla. Mix flour and baking powder, and add alternately with milk. Fold in stiffly beaten egg whites last.

To assemble the cake, grease and flour an oval baking pan. Make a poster-board collar that is about 1 inch smaller than the inside of the pan. Tape the collar together, wrap it with foil or plastic wrap, and place inside of pan. Pour the red batter inside the collar and the white batter outside. Remove the collar and bake the cake at 350 degrees for 25 to 30 minutes. When you slice the cake, cut it into wedges so that they look like watermelon slices, with a white rind and an inner red flesh with seeds.

Orange Wine

48 oranges
5 gallons water
orange peels
10 pounds sugar
1 pint best brandy

Heat the water and pour it over the peels; let this stand for three hours; then add the strained juice of the oranges, then the sugar, and lastly the brandy. Bottle it, and in a few weeks it will be an agreeable beverage.

John Baer's Sons Agricultural Almanac, *1884, Lancaster*

John Baer's Sons promised their customers that their almanacs contained "a variety of useful and entertaining matter." The orange wine recipe may have been more entertaining than useful, as the ingredients required were much too expensive for the average farm family in 1884. Oranges were still considered a luxury item in the nineteenth century, and the child who found an orange on his or her Christmas plate was lucky indeed.

For Making Beer

3 gallons of water

3 lbs of sugar

3 cents crematerter

One quart of molasses

3 cents worth cloves

boil it al together then coleing at colt water milk warm then one quart of yeast in then Ster all together put it in a tup let stan 10 to 12 hours skim ant it makes 8 galons.

Samuel H. Snavely, c. 1860, contributed by Clarke Hess

Landis Valley Museum Collection, PHMC

"In America it's wonderful.
The wine flows in
Through the window.
We drink a bottle wine
And forget Germany."

IMMIGRANT SONG
BY S. F. SAUTER, 1845

AUTHENTIC Recipe Receipt for Beer c. 1900

1 1/2 quarts molasses
3 cts [cents] worth
   Cinamon
1 Table spoonful Cloves
1 pint of sots [liquid yeast]
2 Table spoonfuls Allspice
1 Table spoonful Ginger

1/2 of nutmeg grated on Five gallons of water put all together in a cask and shake it well and put it in the sun and shake it every twenty minutes for ten or 12 hours then put it in a cool cellar for one day or tile settled it is then fit for use.

Mrs. Bentz, c. 1900, contributed by George Roland

AUTHENTIC Recipe Lebkuche (Gingerbread)

3 pounds sugar
4 quarts flour
Saleratus, weight of
   3 copper cents
1 quart thick milk
1 pound butter

Cut into squares, brush with egg, and bake. *Note:* We include this recipe from one of the Lebanon County Historical Society's publications because of the reference to 3 copper cents' worth of saleratus, which was the predecessor of modern baking soda.

"We had fried beef, sweet potatoes, pie,
very nice apple-butter, canned peaches, barley-coffee,
brown sugar, etc. The charge for board was
at the rate of one dollar per day."

PHEBE EARLE GIBBONS, 1873,
WRITING ABOUT A TAVERN NEAR MOUNT JOY,
PENNSYLVANIA, IN 1871

Cherry Tarts like Those Sold in Philadelphia in 1850

2 cups tart cherries,
   pitted and washed
2 or 3 tablespoons flour
dash of nutmeg
1 1/2 cups sugar
hunk of butter
meringue topping
   (see recipe below)

Bring cherries and sugar to a boil about 5 minutes. Mix flour with water to make a smooth paste. Take cherries off the heat and add the paste, put back on stove, and cook until thickened. Add butter and nutmeg. Let cool and then place in baked tart shells. Ice with meringue topping.

Meringue Topping

4 to 6 tablespoons sugar
3 egg whites

Beat egg whites with a whisk until soft peaks form. Gradually add sugar and beat until stiff peaks form. Top cherry tarts with meringue. Heat a salamander or broiler until red hot and brown the tops.

Landis Valley Tavern—complete with the cook!

Dried Corn Chowder

1 cup dried corn
2 quarts water
1 small onion, finely cut
4 large potatoes, diced
1/4 pound bacon, cut up
   in small cubes and fried
1 cup celery, finely cut
1 quart milk
salt and pepper to taste

Place dried corn and water in a large kettle, and bring to a boil. Simmer for about 1 hour. Then add onion, potatoes, celery, and bacon. Simmer about 30 minutes, or until the vegetables are soft. Add milk and simmer until well heated. Add salt and pepper to taste.

Winnie Brendle, contributed by Mrs. Henry Brooks

Fried Cucumbers

Peel large cucumbers and slice lengthwise. Mix 1 cup flour, 1/2 cup yellow cornmeal, and a little salt and pepper. Place in a bowl or on a plate. Beat 1 egg with about 1 tablespoon of water. Dip the cucumber slices in the egg and then in the flour mixture. Fry in a pan of hot lard. Turn over and fry the other side. Serve immediately. Taste is similar to eggplant.

Great Western Almanac, *1843, Philadelphia*

AUTHENTIC Recipe Cream Chockolet Cake

¹/₂ **cup sweet milk**
Yolk of 1 egg
Bring to boil. Cool
1¹/₂ **cups sugar**
¹/₂ **cup sweet milk**
2¹/₂ **cups flour**
1 cup chockolet [cocoa]
¹/₂ **cup sugar**
¹/₂ **cup butter**
1 teaspoon soda

Cream sugar and butter, add eggs and beat well. Add chockolet mixture. Sift flour and soda. Add flour and milk alternately. Place in 2 greased and floured 8-inch pans. Bake at 350 degrees for about 30 minutes.

Jacob Brown, c. 1870–1900, contributed by Clarke Hess

Lemon Sponge Pie

**grated rind and juice
    of 1 lemon**
4 eggs, separated
2 cups sweet milk
2 cups granulated sugar
**2 heaping tablespoons
    flour**
**1 tablespoon melted
    butter**

Mix sugar and flour; then add melted butter and lemon juice and rind. Add well-beaten egg yolks. Blend in the milk and mix well. Beat the egg whites stiff but not dry, and fold into the liquid mixture. Divide between two 8-inch pastry-lined pie dishes. Bake at 435 degrees for 10 minutes. Then turn the oven to 400 degrees and bake 30 to 35 minutes longer. The pies will be dark brown on top. *Helpful hint:* Fill the pies ³/₄ full, place in the oven, and finish filling them in the oven.

Contributed by Emma Shirk

Salad Dressing

7 egg yolks
1 cup hot vinegar
2 cups sweet milk
3 tablespoons flour
2 tablespoons sugar
1 teaspoon salt
1 teaspoon mustard
$1/2$ teaspoon white pepper
1 tablespoon butter

Beat the egg yolks and add sugar, salt, mustard, pepper, and flour. Mix well, add the milk slowly, then the hot vinegar. Cook in a double boiler until the consistency of a very thick cream. Remove from the heat and add butter. Stir until butter is melted and thoroughly mixed. Can be served hot or cold. Refrigerate until ready to use.

Boiled Dressing

2 eggs
1 teaspoon salt
$1/4$ cup melted butter
1 cup vinegar
$1/4$ teaspoon pepper
$1/2$ teaspoon sugar

Beat the eggs lightly without separating; add the vinegar, salt, pepper, sugar, and melted butter. Mix well and put over hot water. Stir constantly until the dressing is thickened; cool and serve. If too thick, thin with cream, as desired. Can be served hot or cold.

Elderberry Pie

Gather elderberries and remove them from the stems. Wash well and drain, and measure approximately 2 cups. Sprinkle with 2 tablespoons of flour. Add 1 cup granulated sugar, 2 tablespoons molasses, and a little lemon juice if desired. Place in an 8-inch pastry-lined shell, dot with butter, and put on a top crust. Bake about 45 minutes to 1 hour. Most fruit pies should start out at 400 degrees and be lowered to 375 degrees after 20 minutes.

Spice Cake

¹/₂ **cup sugar**

¹/₂ **cup milk**

¹/₂ **cup butter**

¹/₂ **teaspoon each cinnamon, cloves, and ginger**

2¹/₂ **cups flour**

¹/₂ **cup molasses**

1 **egg**

¹/₂ **teaspoon baking soda**

Cream butter and sugar. Add the egg and molasses. Blend in the spices. Mix the baking soda with the flour, and add alternately with the milk. Place in a small greased and floured bundt pan. Bake at 350 degrees for about 20 to 25 minutes, or until done.

"Friday 2nd Clear and freezing cold morning with a heavy winter frost, The beans, tomato's, potatoes, pepers, cucumber, squashes &c., were nearly all frozen this morning, some water standing in basins last night, had ice on this morning, the radish leafs had ice on them."

MATTHIAS ZAHM DIARY, LANCASTER, PENNSYLVANIA, JUNE 2, 1843

Brown Flour Potato Soup

3 cups diced potatoes
¹/₂ cup chopped celery
¹/₂ teaspoon celery seed
¹/₂ cup flour
salt and pepper to taste
¹/₂ cup sliced onions
2 hard-boiled eggs
¹/₃ cup butter
1 quart milk
parsley to garnish

Cook the potatoes, onions, and celery in 2 cups water for 10 to 12 minutes. Place the flour in a heavy skillet on medium heat. Stir constantly with a wooden spoon or spatula until flour turns medium brown, not burnt; takes approximately 10 minutes. Add butter and stir until smooth. Remove from heat and add milk slowly, stirring with a whisk. Place back on heat and stir until thoroughly heated. Add cooked potatoes, celery, and onion, plus celery seed, salt, and pepper. Add hard-boiled eggs—sliced or chopped. Garnish with parsley.

Potato Soup

3 cups diced potatoes
1 teaspoon thyme
¹/₂ cup chopped celery
¹/₂ cup finely chopped
   carrots
3 tablespoons flour
salt and pepper to taste
1 bay leaf
1 teaspoon basil
¹/₂ cup chopped onion
2 tablespoons butter
2 hard-boiled eggs, peeled
   and sliced
parsley to garnish

Place potatoes, 2 cups water or chicken stock, herbs, celery, onions, and carrots in a large pot to simmer for about 30 minutes. Remove bay leaf. In a saucepan melt the butter and stir in the flour until smooth. Add some of the cooking liquid, and stir into the flour mixture until thickened. Pour slowly into the soup and stir until thoroughly heated. Add salt and pepper along with the sliced egg. Garnish with parsley. *Optional:* Cook vegetables in a small amount of water and add light cream to make the amount of liquid needed, and then thicken.

Pennsylvania German cooks use a wide variety of herbs and spices. Photo by Michael A. Occhionero

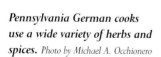

———✖———

*"We were to the hills today in company with I.G. Sensenigs, Sam Sensenigs
& Bro W.W. Hursts. Our refreshments were composed of 2 frezirs ice cream,
ice Lemonade, coffee, Roastin Ears, 2 big cakes, and lots of peaches, pies,
eggs, dry beef, and cheese crackers and many other articles. We were 12
in number strolling around the table which was spread on the ground
under the shady old tree. After dinner the men enjoyed a good smoke while
the women were chattering so noisily that it was impossible for the men
to speak. It was a fine huckle berrie picnic, we got 10 quarts."*

NOAH W. HURST, 1905

Apple Lemonade

6 apples, chopped, with
    stems and blossom
    ends removed (do not
    peel or core)
1½ cups water
cold water
2 cups sugar
3 lemons

Combine apples with 1½ cups water in a covered saucepan and bring to a boil. Reduce heat and simmer until apples are tender, about 20 minutes. Strain apples through a colander lined with two thicknesses of cheesecloth, reserving apple juice. Discard apple pulp. Measure out 2 cups of apple juice, adding a little water if necessary to make the 2 cups. Put juice in a saucepan, add sugar, and place over low heat. Stir until sugar is dissolved. Let cool. Divide the apple syrup equally into six 10-ounce glasses. Squeeze the juice of ½ lemon into each glass. Add ice cubes and fill glasses with cold water. Stir.

Ice Cream Cake

3 egg whites, stiffly beaten
½ cup butter
¾ cup sweet milk
2 teaspoons baking powder
½ cups granulated sugar
2½ cups flour
vanilla to taste

Cream butter and sugar until light and fluffy. Add vanilla. Sift flour and baking powder, and add alternately with milk. Fold in stiffly beaten egg whites. Place in two greased and floured 8-inch cake pans. Bake at 350 degrees for about 30 minutes.

Jacob Brown, c. 1870–1900, contributed by Clarke Hess

 **Ice Cream**

3 pints sweet cream
1 pint pulverized sugar
1 tablespoon vanilla
1 quart milk
The white of 2 eggs
    beaten light

Put in freezer till thoroughly chilled through and then freeze.

Henry H. Landis Ledger, late 1800s

Note: Because of the health risks of using raw eggs, we suggest instead you use meringue powder, available at gourmet food shops. Mix ingredients and put into an ice cream freezer. Turn until thick and chilled. Serve or freeze until ready to use.

Chocolate Cake

1 cup sugar
1 egg
1/4 cup sour milk
1/2 teaspoon vanilla
1/4 cup butter
1/4 cup cocoa
1/2 teaspoon soda
1 cup flour (or a
    little more)

Cream butter and sugar. Add egg. Add vanilla. Sift soda, flour, cocoa, and add alternately with milk. Place in small greased and floured pan. Bake at 350 degrees for about 20 minutes.

Elder Blossom Vine (Wine)

4 pounds white sugar
1 quart picked off
    blossoms
4 quarts water
2 tablespoons yeast
1 lemon

Boil sugar and water together. Let it stand until cool. Pour it over blossoms. Let sit 3 days, and then strain it. Add 1 lemon, sliced, and 2 tablespoons yeast. Ferment 2–3 weeks. Strain off lemon. Pour into gallon jug and cork loosely. When it clears, it is ready—about 6 months.

From a family cookbook, 1903, contributed by Lois Coleman

Walnut Cake

2 cups sugar

4 cups flour

1 cup milk

2 cups walnuts

1 cup butter

4 eggs, separated

1 teaspoon soda

Cream butter and sugar. Add egg yolks. Sift flour and soda, and add alternately with milk. Add stiffly beaten egg whites. Lightly flour walnuts and fold in. Bake in greased and floured pans at 350 degrees for 30 minutes.

Jacob Brown, c. 1870–1900, contributed by Clarke Hess

Marble Cake

Dark Dough:

¹/2 cup brown sugar

2 egg yolks

¹/2 cup dark molasses

¹/4 teaspoon cream of tartar

1 ¹/2 cups all-purpose flour

¹/4 cup butter

¹/4 cup milk

¹/4 teaspoon baking soda

¹/2 teaspoon allspice

¹/4 teaspoon each: cinnamon, cloves, and nutmeg

Light Dough:

¹/2 cup granulated sugar

³/4 cup all-purpose flour

¹/4 teaspoon baking soda

2 egg whites, stiffly beaten

¹/4 cup butter

¹/8 cup milk

¹/4 teaspoon cream of tartar

For the dark dough, cream butter, sugar, and egg yolks. Add molasses. Blend the flour, spices, cream of tartar, and baking soda together, and add alternately with the milk.

For the light dough, cream butter and sugar. Blend flour with baking soda and cream of tartar. Add alternately with the milk. Last of all, fold in stiffly beaten egg whites.

Grease and flour a small bundt pan or a 9-inch cake pan. Alternate the two doughs and swirl around in the pan to make a marbleized effect. Bake in a 350-degree oven for 25 to 30 minutes.

Lemon Ice Cream

rind of 1 lemon
juice of 1 1/2 lemons
1 cup sugar
2 pints heavy whipping
   cream

Grate the rind of a lemon into a bowl and set aside. Squeeze the juice of 1 1/2 lemons into a cup, and put through a fine sieve to get rid of pulp and seeds. Add juice to the rind. Place the juice, rind, and sugar in a stainless steel bowl of about 3- to 4-quart size, with a tight-fitting plastic lid. Stir well to try to dissolve the sugar. Then add the heavy cream. Stir until sugar is completely dissolved. Put some ice and ice cream salt in a large stainless dishpan. Put the lid tightly on the bowl, and nest it in the larger bowl of ice. Pile more ice and salt around the bowl until it is completely surrounded. Be sure the bowl is well seated in the ice and salt mixture. Now with your fingers, start to revolve the bowl in the ice. After about 5 to 7 minutes, take off the lid, and scrape the bottom and sides of the bowl with a heavy spoon. The ice cream should be freezing fast to the bowl; you are scraping the frozen ice cream to the center so that more ice cream can freeze to the bowl. Put the lid back on and continue to turn for another 3 to 5 minutes, then remove the lid and scrape the sides again. Continue to do this until all the ice cream is frozen. It shouldn't take more than about 20 minutes, if you have enough salt mixed in with the ice. The ice cream can remain in this ice-salt mixture for about 1 hour to keep it frozen until ready to serve. If longer than that, place in your home freezer. This is a very wonderful ice cream and extremely rich. Most folks won't eat more than a tablespoon or two.

Cherry Bounce

2 quarts cherries, sweet or
   sour, or a combination
   of both kinds
2 pounds sugar
2 fifths good whiskey

Place cherries, sugar, and whiskey in a large gallon jug, and shake it every day for a month. Let sit until Thanksgiving or about two weeks before Christmas. Strain off the cherries and bottle. It is a good Christmas drink. *Note:* It is not necessary to pit or crush the cherries. You can, if desired, but then it produces more sediment and needs to be strained more.

Apricot Ice Cream

1 pound fresh apricots
1 cup sugar
2 pints heavy whipping
   cream

Cut the apricots up into small pieces, and then mash with a masher. Add sugar and stir well. Now add cream and freeze as in above recipe. *Note:* Because apricots are not in season very long, you can use 1 can of apricots instead of fresh ones. Drain off juice and smash apricots. Add only about $1/2$ cup sugar and mix with the cream. Freeze as above.

Both of these ice cream recipes date from the early 1800s. The freezing method is just as the Pennsylvania Germans did with the sourboughteer, a wooden tub with a tight-lidded metal can that sat in the tub full of salt and ice. This can was turned to rotate the contents.

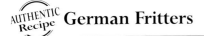 ## German Fritters

Take some well-tarted crisp apples. Pare, quarter and core them. Put into a stew pan one fourth pint of French Brandy, a table-spoon of sugar, and a little cinnamon. Put the apples in the brandy and cook slowly, stirring often, but not breaking up the apples. Set another pan on the fire with a couple of tablespoons of lard. When hot, drain the apples and flour them. Put them on the fire. Put sugar over the apples and glaze them over top with a red hot salamander.

Modern Domestic Cookery and Useful Receipt Book, *1828*

Note: A salamander was a long-handled heavy iron disk-like pad-dle used to brown foods. It was heated until it glowed red and held 2 inches above the food to be browned.

Boiled, unpeeled potatoes are potatoes with the jackets on.

PENNSYLVANIA GERMAN FOLKLORE

Soft Pretzels

2 1/4 **cups warm water**
1 **tablespoon salt**
4 **to** 5 **cups flour**
1/2 **cup brown sugar**
1 **packet yeast**

Mix water, brown sugar, and salt together. Dissolve yeast and add the flour to make a moderately stiff dough. Knead well until very smooth and satiny. Let rise about 1 hour. Punch down the dough and divide into about 18 to 20 pieces. Let rest a few minutes. Meanwhile, in a large shallow kettle, mix 1 tablespoon of baking soda into 1 gallon of water, and bring to just under the boiling point. Roll out the dough into long ropes about 24 inches in length. Twist into pretzel shapes. By the time you have all the pretzels shaped, you can start placing them in the simmering

water solution, 3 or 4 pretzels at a time. Leave them in about 1 minute, then take out and drain on towels. Place on lightly greased baking sheets, and cover the pretzels with pretzel salt or kosher salt. Bake in a hot oven at 400 degrees for about 10 minutes. Serve immediately.

To dry pretzels for Christmas decorations, place them on a cookie sheet and let dry several hours or overnight in a barely warm oven of about 100 to 150 degrees. They will last several months if well dried. Attach strings or yarn and hang on your Christmas tree.

UTHENTIC Recipe For Making Indian Cakes, or Pones

To one quart of milk add three eggs—beat them well—then add as much meal as will make a batter of the same consistency as is used for buckwheat cakes, pour into a bake kettle and bake as for other cakes. When sour milk can be had it is preferred, into which put some pearlash, as for baking biscuits.

When cakes are made according to the above directions, most people prefer them to wheat bread, and no doubt they are healthier. They should be eaten warm and with a cup of coffee make an excellent breakfast. In addition to all their recommendations, they are economical.

Baer's Almanac, 1835, Lancaster, Pennsylvania

Note: Pearlash is an eighteenth-century leavening that was first used commercially in bakeries, and then found its way into homes. It probably was used into the 1840s. As the name implies, it is a by-product of wood ash. We have used pearlash in our cooking demonstrations at Landis Valley Museum. It must be well dissolved in a little water or milk and used immediately. Otherwise, it can make black streaks and leave a bitter taste, and it can lose strength if it sits too long.

Corn Bread
(as prepared at Landis Valley Museum)

2 cups buttermilk
1/4 cup granulated sugar
2 cups cornmeal
2 eggs
1 teaspoon baking soda
1 cup flour

Beat the eggs; add buttermilk, sugar, and baking soda. Add flour and cornmeal, and mix until smooth. Pour into a well-greased Dutch oven that has been preheated. Bake about 20 minutes. Or pour into a greased pan and bake at 350 degrees for 25 to 30 minutes.

Harvest Home
Giving Thanks

A fall Harvest Home bounty.

*"Thanksgiving is beginning to be observed here,
but the New Englander would miss the family gatherings,
the roast turkeys, the pumpkins, we do not greatly fancy them.
Raisin-pie, or mince-pie, we can enjoy."*

PHEBE EARLE GIBBONS, 1874

To make strong vinegar,
speak the names of the
three most evil women
you know into the bung
hole before you close it.

A Personal Memory by Dawn L. Fetter

New England had their Thanksgiving, but the Pennsylvania Dutch had Harvest Home. Harvest Home was a church festival celebrating the end of harvest season. It truly was a time to share one's wealth and give thanks. Members of the congregation decorated the church very elaborately with the bounty of the harvest. Tiers were made to display home-canned goods. Glass jars glowed with the colors of peaches, pears, cherries, green and yellow string beans, pickles, red beets, and chow chow. Interspersed among the canned goods were fresh apples, pears, cabbages, endive, pumpkins, squash, and lots of flowers.

Before money was readily available to pay the ministers a full salary, they were paid with fruits and vegetables, and even flowers. Once ministers were better paid, this bounty was given to orphanages, church homes, and needy people.

As a little girl attending Swamp Church in northern Lancaster County, I was so amazed at the decorations around the communion rail. Swamp Church is between Reinholds and Blainsport, Pennsylvania. Both the Reformed and Lutheran congregations used the church. One week we would attend our Reformed service, and the next week we'd go to the Lutheran service.

For the Harvest Home festival, we always sat in the front row of the balcony so we could look down on it all. It was so beautiful. Corn shocks were used in back of the tiers and around the

---

"Finished Cider. Boiled 27 crocks
of apple butter and prepared for market.
Cost of apple butter $8.00."

PETER C. HILLER DIARY, SEPTEMBER 7, 1883

Haystacks near Hamburg,
Berks County, c. 1905.
Mr. and Mrs. Michael Emery

"Gathered about 12 qts of chestnuts by shaking three trees and husked a bushel basket of corn for the pigs."

PETER C. HILLER DIARY,
OCTOBER 4, 1879

sides. Baskets of red, gold, and yellow flowers were placed among the canned goods, as well as cabbage, apples, and endive. On the floor were baskets of sweet potatoes, potatoes, red beets, nuts, apples, pears, and anything else that could be put into them. To add more color, there were pumpkins, squash, ears of corn, and even more flowers.

Because I liked to sing, I thought the best part were the hymns that we sang. All referred to harvest time. The one I remember the best was "Bringing In the Sheaves."

Some churches still have a harvest service, but most are not decorated anymore. This is one tradition that I wish my grandchildren could have seen.

Cucumber Relish

1 peck cucumbers
3 cups sugar
2 tablespoons mustard
    seed
6 large onions
1 tablespoon celery seed
3 cups vinegar

Pare and grind cucumbers and onions. Sprinkle salt over mixture and let stand 1 hour. Drain. Combine sugar and spices with vinegar, and pour over vegetables. Cook for 25 minutes. Add 3 cloves and 3 allspice to each full kettle. Pour into jars and seal.

Grandmother's recipe, 1910, contributed by Margaret Sheaffer

Pepper Cabbage

1 small head of cabbage
pinch of salt
$1/2$ cup water
1 small bell pepper, any
    color
$3/4$ cup granulated sugar
$1/2$ cup cider vinegar

Take cabbage and cut in half; then shred it fine, using coarse holes on a four-sided cutter. Add a pinch of salt and set aside. Remove the seeds from a bell pepper; then dice it fairly fine. Toss cabbage and peppers together. Then mix sugar, water, and cider vinegar together. Stir well to dissolve sugar. Mix the liquid and cabbage together. Refrigerate. Serve anytime.

Molasses Cakes

1 cup dark molasses
   (New Orleans)
2 tablespoons baking soda
1 cup granulated sugar
2 eggs
$1/2$ cup soft lard
1 cup sweet milk
enough flour to make stiff,
   about $4^{1}/2$ cups

Mix together molasses and baking soda, and dissolve soda in the molasses. Add the remaining ingredients to the molasses mixture. Drop by tablespoons on a slightly greased baking sheet. Egg wash the tops of the cookies with 1 egg beaten with 1 tablespoon of water, and sprinkle with sugar. Bake at 350 degrees for 10 to 12 minutes.

Contributed by Linda Brubaker

 ## To Pickle French Beans

Take young slender fresh Beans, then make a Brine with cold Water & salt strong enough to bear en Egg put your Beans into that Brine & let them lie fourteen Days then take them out & wash them in fair Water & set them on the fire in cold Water without salt & let them boil or rather simmer until they are tender then throw them into Cold Water & when they are cold drain them from their Water & make a Pickle for them, to a Peck of French Beans you must have a Gallon of Vinegar boil it with some Mace whole pepper & sliced ginger then put your Beans into a Jar & pour the Pickle boiling hot over them.

Sarah Yeates Cookbook, *1767–1829*

Spiced Peaches

7 pounds peaches
1 quart vinegar
1 tablespoon cinnamon
3 cinnamon sticks
4 pounds brown sugar
1 teaspoon whole cloves
1 teaspoon whole allspice

Tie the spices in a bag and boil with the vinegar. Stir in the sugar and keep stirring until dissolved. Scald and peel the peaches, but leave them whole, including the pits. Drop them, a few at a time, into the syrup, and cook until tender but not soft. Pack into hot jars and seal.

Green Tomato Chutney

4 cups green tomatoes,
  peeled and chopped
  into cubes

2 cups seedless raisins,
  chopped

1 cup onions, peeled and
  chopped fine

3 cloves garlic, peeled and
  minced

1 tablespoon salt

1 tablespoon mustard seed

3 cups hard green apples,
  chopped fine

$^1/_3$ cup candied ginger,
  chopped fine

$^1/_2$ cup sweet pepper,
  chopped

2 cups brown sugar

$^1/_2$ teaspoon mace

2 cups good cider vinegar

Mix everything well; then bring to a boil and simmer 30 minutes. Stir often or this will stick to the pan. Pack into clean, hot jars and seal.

Ketchup

1 peck tomatoes
  ($^1/_2$ peach basket)

2 large onions

2 tablespoons Coleman's
  dry mustard

1 cup sugar

1 pint vinegar

4 tablespoon black pepper

2 tablespoons whole
  cloves, 1 teaspoon dry
  red pepper, and 2 sticks
  cinnamon, tied into
  cheesecloth

Quarter tomatoes, leaving skins on. Boil with the onions for 2 hours. Put through strainer, and return pulp to a large pot. Add other ingredients and slowly boil for 3 hours. Skim off the scum that forms on top. Remove spice bag. Boil bottles or jars, fill, and seal.

Baked Pears

Pare twelve large baking pears, and cut them into halves, leaving on the stem about half an inch long. Take out the cores with the point of a knife, and place halves close together in a black tin saucepan with a bright inside, with a cover that fits quite close. Add the rind of a lemon, cut thin, with half its juice, a small stick of cinnamon, and twenty grains of allspice. Cover them with spring water, allowing 1 pound of loaf sugar to 1 1/2 pints of water. Cover them and bake 6 hours in a very slow oven. Pears will be quite tender and of a bright color. *Note:* Prepared cochineal is generally used for coloring the pears, but if the above is strictly attended to, it will be found to work well.

 ## Cider Cake

Take two pounds of flour, one pound of sugar, one and one half pound of butter, one pint of cider, cloves and cinnamon, with or without fruit, two teaspoons of pearlash [an early leavening].

Brother Jonathon's Almanac, *1862, Philadelphia*

Cider Cake (Modern Version)

2 cups flour
1/2 cup cider
1 teaspoon cinnamon
1/2 teaspoon baking soda
1/2 cup brown sugar
3/4 cup butter
dash of cloves
1/2 cup raisins

Cream butter and sugar, and add spices. Mix and sift the flour and baking soda; add to butter mixture alternately with the cider. Fold in the raisins. Spoon into a greased 9-inch cake pan. Bake at 350 degrees for about 25 to 30 minutes.

*A **cider press.** Landis Valley Museum Collection, PHMC*

Fried Rabbit

1 rabbit
salted water for soaking
^{1}/4 cup flour
salt and pepper
^{1}/4 cup lard or butter
1 tablespoon flour
1 cup water

Clean rabbit and cut into pieces for frying. Soak in salt water 8 to 10 hours. Remove from water, drain, and dredge in ^{1}/4 cup flour. Place in hot skillet containing the lard or butter. Cover and fry to a golden brown, turning frequently. Season with salt and pepper. To make gravy, remove the rabbit to a hot platter when finished frying, and stir 1 tablespoon flour into the hot grease. Add 1 cup water and cook until mixture thickens.

Pork and Chicken Soup

4 to 5 pounds stewing chicken
2 or 3 small carrots
2 cups rice, brown or white
^{1}/2 pound slab bacon
3 onions
salt and pepper to taste

Wash the chicken well and remove excess fat. Put in a large kettle, cover with water, and bring to a boil. Boil until tender. Meanwhile, cut the bacon into small cubes and fry until crisp and brown. Drain the bacon, reserving the grease. Chop the onions fine and fry in the bacon grease. Drain and set aside. Remove the chicken from the broth and allow to cool. Discard the chicken skin and cut the chicken into bite-size pieces. Set aside. Finely dice the carrots and add to the chicken broth. Add the rice and cook according to package directions, until it is tender. Usually white rice takes about 20 minutes and brown rice takes about 45 minutes to cook. About 10 minutes before rice is done, add the chicken, bacon, and onions. Add salt and pepper to taste. Serves 4 to 6.

Potato Soup

6 or 8 medium potatoes
^{1}/2 pound slab of bacon
2 stalks celery
2 tablespoons parsley
3 medium onions
1 tablespoon flour
2 or 3 leeks
salt and pepper to taste

Peel the potatoes and slice thin. Dice the celery and add to the potatoes. Place in a kettle, cover with water, and boil until soft. Meanwhile, dice the bacon and fry in a pan. Drain the bacon, reserving the fat. Dice the onions fine and slice the leeks. Fry in the bacon fat until lightly browned. Drain off excess fat, and add the bacon, onions, and leeks to the potatoes. Sprinkle in the flour and parsley, and add salt and pepper to taste. Cook just a few minutes more, until slightly thickened. Serve over toasted, buttered bread cubes.

Der Deutcshes Hausfrau Kochbuch, *1894*

Grape Butter

4 cups Concord grapes
4 cups granulated sugar

Pick the grapes off the stems and wash well. Measure 4 cups. Mash the grapes in a large preserving kettle, add the sugar, and bring to a boil. Boil 20 minutes. Run the mixture through a sieve and put into jelly glasses. Seal with wax when cooled.

Apple Butter

20 gallons cider
1 1/2 bushels of apples
(applesauce type,
such as smokehouse
or McIntosh)
15 to 20 pounds sugar
spices as desired

The night before cooking the apple butter, have a snitzing party to peel, core, and quarter the apples. Early the next morning, start a wood fire, and while the fire is burning, clean your apple butter kettle. It should be a 30-gallon copper kettle. It needs to be thoroughly cleaned with vinegar and salt and scrubbed until shiny. *Never use an iron kettle; the iron will leach out and turn the apple butter black, making it unfit for use.* Set your kettle over the fire and pour in the cider. Cook for several hours, until it has been reduced to about half the volume. Stir occasionally. *You must use a wooden paddle-type stirrer.* Add the apples gradually. Once the apples go in, the mixture must be stirred constantly. If it burns, the apple butter is ruined. When it starts to turn a nice light brown color, add some sugar. Taste it and sweeten to your taste. Test the apple butter for doneness by placing some on a saucer and immediately turning the saucer upside down. If it doesn't fall off the plate, it's done. Another method is to put some on a saucer and let it sit until it's cooled off. If no cider or liquid separates from the apple butter, it's done. Add spices just before removing from the fire. Keep stirring even as you remove it from the fire. Stir until it stops cooking. Place in 1-gallon crocks. Recipe should make 10 to 12 gallons. It takes a lot of firewood and a lot of cooking. Total cooking time should be about 8 to 10 hours, depending on the quality of the firewood and how hot the fire is.

Quince Honey

1 cup peeled and grated
   quinces (about 6 to
   8 quinces)
3 cups water
2 cups sugar

Mix grated quinces, water, and sugar. Bring to a boil, and boil until thickened. Place in hot jelly glasses and seal.

Aunt Anna Hess, 1930s, contributed by Joan Pyott

Dried Fruit Pies

For pear, schnitz (dried apple), and apricot pies, soak the fruit several hours or overnight. Place on the stove and bring to a boil. For 3 cups of fruit (after it has been soaked), mix 3/4 cup brown sugar and 2 tablespoons flour, and stir into the fruit mixture. Boil until thickened. Add spices if desired. For schnitz pie, add cinnamon and just a small dash of cloves. Always taste the pie filling and add more sugar if desired. Let cool thoroughly and place into a pastry-lined pie dish. Dot with butter, put on a top crust, and bake at 400 degrees for 40 to 45 minutes.

Stone Fence Punch

1 quart applejack or rum
1 orange, sliced
2 quarts sweet cider
10 to 15 whole cloves

This punch was a favorite with farm workers at the turn of the nineteenth century. It was concocted of sweet cider and applejack or rum. It is a rather potent drink, as the quantity of applejack indicates.

Combine the applejack or rum and cider in a punch bowl with a large chunk of ice or molded ice ring. Garnish with orange slices, each studded with a few cloves. Yields 3 quarts. For an individual serving, put 2 jiggers of applejack or rum into a highball glass. Add 2 ice cubes, and fill the glass with sweet cider. A twist of lemon or orange peel adds flavor and color.

Susie Riehl's Pumpkin Pie

1 cup fresh cooked
   pumpkin
1/2 cup milk
2 eggs
1 1/2 teaspoons cinnamon
1/4 teaspoon each nutmeg,
   allspice, and ginger
1/2 cup granulated sugar
1 tablespoon flour
2 tablespoons molasses
   (King Syrup)
dash of cloves

Mix sugar and flour, and add the spices. Next, add the eggs and pumpkin. Last, add molasses and milk. Place in one large 9-inch pastry-lined pie shell. Bake at 400 degrees for about 45 minutes.

Chicken Terrapin

Cut up a cold roasted chicken in very small pieces, being careful to remove all pieces of skin. Put in a skillet with a tumbler full of cream and a good-size piece of butter rolled in flour. Season with a little mustard, a teaspoonful of salt, a small pinch of cayenne pepper, ground cloves, nutmeg, and mace. Have ready three hard-boiled eggs cut in small pieces and one wineglass full of wine. When the chicken has come to a boil, stir in the egg. Remove from the stove and add the wine. Put back over the heat and stir for a few minutes. Serve at once.

H.S. Forry, 1905

"The year 1844 is the greatest year for all kinds of fruit;
apricots, plums, gauges, apples, peaches.
Pears are in such abundance that people scarcely
know how to dispose of them.
. . . Apples were offered in market
at Lancaster for 10 cts per bushel."

MATTHIAS ZAHM DIARY,
LANCASTER, PA, OCTOBER 2, 1844

CHAPTER 8

Butchering Day
You Can Use All of the Pig Except the Oink

One of our favorite residents of Landis Valley Museum.

"Butchering is one of the many occasions for the display of friendly feeling, when brother or father steps in to help hang the hogs, or a sister to assist in rendering lard or in preparing a plentiful meal. . . . The friends who have assisted receive a portion of the sausage, etc., which portion is called the 'metzel-sup.' The 'metzel-sup' is also sent to poor widows and others."

PHEBE EARLE GIBBONS, 1874

A Personal Memory by Jerri Horner

My mother and uncle Bill loved butchering day. The pig and I hated it. Obviously, you can understand why the pig felt that way. My feelings were more complex but just as selfish.

Butchering was always done on a cold day, usually just after Thanksgiving in our Cambria County home. The time period was the 1950s, but butchering methods had changed little over the centuries. We used a gas stove, whereas our ancestors used wood fires. And our meat was frozen instead of smoked or pickled.

Mom would awaken me before daybreak with enthusiasm and urge me to hurry and join the excitement. Pulling my reluctant body from the warm cocoon and forcing it into the cold morning air, where my fingers became chapped as we scraped hair from a dead pig carcass, wasn't my idea of fun.

At least the worst was over by the time I forced myself outside.

A local butcher arrives with a delivery.
Landis Valley Museum Collection, PHMC

Butchering the Pig

Uncle Bill did the actual killing using a bullet to the head. He felt that was the most humane method and had no patience for those who clobbered their animals on the head with a hammer. The pig was hoisted up by block and tackle until it hung head-down from a large tripod.

The pig was bled quickly by slitting its throat. Then it was scalded in hot water to make hair removal easier. Sometimes lye or ashes were added to the water to hasten removal of the bristles. Scraping the hog bristles off was a job usually assigned to the children. We had no actual scrapers. Mom saved all the old rusty rings from canning jars, and we used them.

After the hair was scraped and shaved off, the carcass was hoisted up again and the pig was gutted. The liver and heart were saved to add to the pudding pot. The intestines were saved for casing, and the stomach was saved to stuff and eat. We children blew up the bladder and tossed it around like a balloon. (In much earlier times, the bladder was stretched over the tops of crocks of pickles as a seal.) Another butchering day joke was to pin the pigtail on an unsuspecting victim.

After gutting the pig, the head and feet were cut off. Then men split the carcass down the backbone. They made additional cuts until the pork pieces were small enough to handle. These pieces were taken inside for mom to cut into

The Pennsylvania Germans raised many pigs, as pork was a favored meat. Landis Valley Museum Collection, PHMC

meal-size portions and package for the freezer. Parts not being packaged immediately were left outside to chill in the cold November air.

Cooking the Pig

My mother put the liver and heart into a pot with water, bones, and small scraps of pork and boiled them. When cooled in pans or dishes, this mixture was called meat pudding. My dad liked this spread on crackers or heated and cooked with potatoes and onions.

By adding cornmeal and flour or buckwheat meal, we made Pannhaas (scrapple).

We used the terms Pannhaas and scrapple interchangeably to mean the same thing, although some people felt that scrapple had more meat, and Pannhaas was made with the broth only.

Mom was fussy about what went into the pudding broth. "No ears, eyeballs, or gristle," she insisted. "I don't like gristle in my pannhaas." She also fussed if any stray pig hairs accidentally made it into the pot. We seasoned our scrapple with salt and pepper only.

All fat was saved and rendered (melted down) to make lard. The crunchy fat left after rendering was called cracklins and eaten as a snack. Nobody knew anything about cholesterol back then. Lard was used in cooking, frying, and baking, as well as in seasoning the old cast-iron cookware. Also, before canning became popular, a layer of lard was put over cooked sausage in a crock to help preserve it. It was common for a Pennsylvania Dutchman to brag about how many crocks or cans of lard his hog had provided.

We never made blood pudding, but Uncle Bill liked to make head cheese and pickled pig's

feet. I think he even made tongue souse. Head cheese and souse consist of bits of cooked meat in a gelatinlike substance, similar to today's lunch meats. Though he died long ago, I can still picture Uncle Bill with a pig's head tucked under his arm as he left our house on butchering day. A tall, thin man, Bill and that head made quite a picture.

Uncle Bill always received a portion of the meat, plus the head and feet, in exchange for his help. It wasn't until I began working at Landis Valley Museum and researched butchering day that I realized this custom was handed down to us by our early ancestors. Called metzelsupp, or butcher's soup, the offering began as a soup to feed the helpers. Often it was laced with whiskey, and rye bread was broken into it. This custom evolved into the more modern tradition of presenting a portion of the meat, often sausages and spareribs, to the helpers.

Using the Other Parts

In the early 1800s and later, the children saved the pig bristles, cleaning and sorting them, and selling them to brushmakers and storekeepers. We discarded them.

One of the worst tasks of the day fell to Mom. She would clean the intestines to use as casings to hold the sausage. Taking a dull knife, she turned them inside out and scraped them clean on a smooth board. When clean, she soaked them in salt water and chilled them until needed.

Our family had a large sausage stuffer mounted on a board about 10 inches wide and 3 to 4 feet long. This was placed across two wooden kitchen chairs. A young child sat on each end of the board, weighing it down enough for the older children to operate the stuffer.

The butchering process.
Photos by Bruce Light

One of the older kids threaded the casings onto a metal nozzle that projected from the bottom of the large cylinder that held the sausage. As one child slowly turned the handle, the lid inside the cylinder pressed down the meat and forced it into the casings. Casings frequently broke, causing us to utter words that were sure to bring threats from Mom if she chanced to hear them. Not only did this process get the sausage links made, but it also kept four kids away from the sharp butchering knives Mom was using to cut the meat.

The meal that night was always fresh pork chops rimmed with Schpeck (fat). Mom was ecstatic knowing that she had enough meat to feed her family for the long winter ahead.

I always chose to eat vegetables instead.

The pig was hoisted.

The Butchering Process

Many hands were kept busy on butchering day. The pig had to be killed, bled, hung, put into scalding water, have the hair removed, and be gutted. The intestines were cleaned for sausage casing.

Butcher when the moon is waxing so the meat doesn't shrink.

<small>PENNSYLVANIA GERMAN
FOLKLORE</small>

Scalding the pig.

"My mom always cleaned the pig bladder and stuffed it with sausage. Then it was put in a muslin bag and hung in the smokehouse and smoked. That was our break-fast sausage. It was sliced and fried."

IRVEN "PEPS" REINARD, 1999

Head and feet cut off, and split.

Cleaning the casings.

I can still picture Uncle Bill with a pig's head tucked under his arm.

Scrapple (Pannhaas)

2 pig hearts
2 pounds semifatty pork
3 cups yellow cornmeal
1 cup buckwheat flour
2 tablespoons black
    pepper
1$^{1}/_{2}$ pounds pig liver
2 or 3 pounds pork bones
    (optional)
$^{1}/_{2}$ cup flour
2 tablespoons salt
1$^{1}/_{2}$ tablespoons ground
    sage (optional)

Cover all bones and meat completely with water, and boil for 3 hours. Remove the meat and bones; let cool. Strain the liquid and set aside. Cut excess fat and gristle off the meat, and discard the bones. Grind the meat. Mix flour, buckwheat flour, and cornmeal. Dissolve the flour mixture in some of the liquid to make a smooth paste. Add it to the rest of the liquid and meat, and put on the stove to boil. When it comes to a boil, take it off the fire and stir in the flour-cornmeal mixture. Return to the heat and boil for about 30 to 45 minutes or until very thick. The mixture must be stirred constantly when the cornmeal mixture is added, as it will burn very easily. It is said to be ready to pour in pans when a broomstick remains upright in the mixture. Pour scrapple into bread pans. Let cool, refrigerate overnight, and the scrapple will be ready to fry. If it is cooked nice and thick, it will slice easily and fry without falling apart. Fry in a skillet with a little lard and butter. Cook on both sides. Some people dip the scrapple in flour before frying; others do not. Salt, pepper, and sage can be added when the cornmeal mixture is added to the meat broth. Taste the mixture and add more seasonings if necessary. Sage is optional; some prefer just salt and pepper.

Sausage Casings and Using a Sausage Gun

"About 4 o'clock in the morning, old Overlustig's at the sighn of the red lion, or cat, in Prince street, burnd with all his meat in smoke house."

MATTHIAS ZAHM DIARY, LANCASTER, PENNSYLVANIA, MARCH 2, 1821

Purchase clean sausage casings, or prepare your own by scraping and cleaning the pig intestines. Rinse them well and place in a pan of warm water to keep pliable. The inside of the sausage gun and the exterior nozzle should be slightly greased with a little lard. Find the opening of a casing and thread it onto the exterior nozzle. Keep it centered. Try not to jab holes in the casing. Tie the casing with linen thread or knot it. Insert the plunger and start pushing to force the meat into the casing. Hold the plunger against your breastbone for added force. It is helpful to have another person hold the casing and guide it for even filling. When you come to the end of a casing, tie it off. The casings should be used as soon as possible. If a casing dries on the nozzle, it won't fill properly. Don't remove the casings from the water until ready to use. When done, take the sausage gun apart, wash it well, and allow to dry. *Do not* put the plunger back into the stuffer until it is thoroughly dry, usually the next day.

Bratwurst (Brotwascht)

5 pounds coarsely ground pork

1 pound coarsely ground bacon

1 medium ground onion

3 tablespoons coarse salt

2 tablespoons black pepper

1 teaspoon ground cloves

1 tablespoon sage

2 cups water

1 tablespoon marjoram

1 tablespoon ginger

2 tablespoons ground coriander

Mix the ground meat and onion together. Mix the water, salt, pepper, and spices together. Using your hands, mix all ingredients together. Place in a sausage stuffer and stuff the casings.

Photo by Bruce Light

Pig Stomach (Seimaage)

1 pig stomach, cleaned
   and rinsed

5 pounds potatoes,
   cut into cubes

salt

2 pounds sausage, no skin

small onion, diced

Mix ingredients. Stuff pig stomach. Bake at 350 degrees for
3 hours.

Mabel Z. (Nanny) Young, 1920, contributed by Helen Young Meckley

Preparing the pig stomach.

 ## Sausage

To every 12 pounds of meat add 3 tablespoons salt not much heaped, 3 tablespoons of black pepper, and 8 tablespoons of sage. Mix well and put into casings.

John Baer's Almanac, *1864, Lancaster, Pennsylvania*

Note: We at the museum found that it required a little more salt and pepper, but only about 5 tablespoons of sage.

To Cure Pork

For 80 pounds of pork take 3 ounces saltpeter, $1/2$ pound sugar (brown), 1 pint fine salt, then let it lay 48 hours. Then add 2 quarts fine salt to it then let it lay 3 weeks. Then you can smoke it. (Take the first three ingredients and mix it together and rub it into your hams. In 48 hours rub in another 2 quarts of salt and let lay three weeks. Then smoke your hams.) Note: If trying this recipe the meat must be kept cold like in a cold cellar, etc. It is usually laid on boards. Turn the hams occasionally. *Never use iodized salt to preserve any meat. It will not keep.*

Mary Stoner, 1864, contributed by Clarke Hess

Sausage Cooked in Cider

Place $1 1/2$ pounds of fresh pork sausage in a large frying pan, and add about 2 cups of fresh apple cider to the pan. Cook slowly, turning the sausage often, until the cider becomes brown and syrupy. Add more cider if necessary. Makes a wonderfully sweet and tasty sausage. Will take about 45 minutes to 1 hour to cook.

He comes to the trough hungry and eats himself full.

PENNSYLVANIA GERMAN
FOLKLORE

Head Cheese

Clean a hog's head well, and remove the eyes and brain. Put in a large kettle and cover with water. Boil until the meat falls from the bone. Remove from the fire and allow to cool. Remove the bones. For each gallon of meat, add 1 tablespoon pepper, 2 teaspoons sage, and 1 teaspoon salt. Squeeze all the meat together, place in a dish or pan, and allow to set until solid. Slice and serve.

Pig's Feet Souse

Soak 2 sets of pig's feet in cold water for 2 hours. Clean thoroughly. Put in pot and cover with 3 quarts water. Simmer until tender, several hours or so. Remove the meat from the bones, but keep it in large pieces. Bring to a boil 1 cup of cider vinegar and 1 teaspoon allspice. Put the meat into a dish, and season with salt and pepper to taste. Cover with the vinegar mixture and allow to cool completely.

Never butcher on Ember Day or the meat will spoil.
[Ember Days are three days in each season reserved
for prayer and fasting by certain Christian churches.]

PENNSYLVANIA GERMAN FOLKLORE

CHAPTER 9

Christmas
Christkindl and Belsnickel

"One and only one Kriss-kringle with horrid mask on made his appearance to-night in the store, much to the affright of the several youngsters of the family."

JAMES L. MORRIS DIARY,
DECEMBER 24 1846,
*THE PENNSYLVANIA
DUTCHMAN,* 1952

Christmas celebrations of today and yesterday are as different as toads from turnips—or, more appropriately, as Belsnickel from Santa Claus.

Little is known of American Christmas customs before the early 1800s. Many may not have celebrated the day at all. Those who did perceived it as a religious holiday. How Pennsylvania Germans marked the day greatly depended upon their religious beliefs.

Of all the Pennsylvania German religious groups, the Protestant Moravians had the earliest and most elaborate Christmas celebrations. Moravians introduced the putz, a Christmas scene made of moss, clay figures, fences, and animals. From trombone choirs to love feasts with sugar cakes and coffee, the Moravians celebrated Christ's birthday with joy and music and festivities.

Not all religious groups had fancy Christmas celebrations then, nor do they today. Many of the conservative Pennsylvania Germans, such as the Amish and Mennonites, may have marked the day with a large dinner at most. By the late 1800s, however, many in the Pennsylvania Dutch culture, including the Lutheran and German Reformed, had opted for the pageantry and extensive decorations that we now associate with the modern Christmas holiday. Many Pennsylvania German Protestants created elaborate Christmas scenes that filled entire rooms in their homes.

One of the earliest records of a Christmas tree appears in Matthias Zahm's diary of 1821, where Zahm, of Lancaster, Pennsylvania, wrote, "Sally and our Thos. And Wm. Hensel was out for Christmas trees, on the hill at Kendrick's saw mill."

Early decorations, often homemade, were simple ones such as cookies, pretzels, march pane (marzipan), and apple schnitz (dried apple slices). Notice that they are all foods. To many Pennsylvania Dutch, Christmas meant three things: the Christ Child, Belsnickel, and food! Some early Christmas trees were hung from the ceiling beams to avoid using floor space and to protect the edible decorations from rats and mice.

The weeks prior to Christmas were hectic ones for our ancestors, as they are for us today. Days were filled with butchering hogs and filling wash baskets with cookies. Often the first hogs of the season were butchered just before Christmas. Friends and neighbors came to help as well as to socialize and share the Metzelsupp, a soup made of meat scraps, bread, and whiskey. Since so many overindulged and became quite drunk, eventually this practice was discontinued. Instead, helpers received some of the fresh meat. Children earned money to buy Christmas candy, such as Mooschi and bellyguts (pulled taffy), by selling cleaned hog bristles to the brushmakers.

With fresh pork available, it was natural to serve stuffed pig stomach for Christmas dinner.

Cookie baking in the Tavern at Landis Valley Museum. Photo by Stephany Molenko

The women cleaned the stomach well, washed it in salt, and stuffed it with a mixture of potatoes, onions, and sausage. The stomach was boiled for several hours, and then browned in butter or lard just before serving. Sometimes it was roasted in a Dutch oven or bake oven.

In some areas, families enjoyed goose or turkey with sauerkraut as the main dish. The bird was stuffed with kraut and roasted in a Dutch oven for several hours, making a tasty meal.

The Christ Plate

We'd hardly recognize our ancestors' gifts as such. Most were simple things such as a handful of apple schnitz, a few cookies, or a piece of candy. Children placed bread baskets or plates on the kitchen table and found food gifts on them in the morning. They believed that the Christ Child had come through the keyhole during the night to deliver these gifts. The custom was known as "setting the Christ plates."

By the late 1800s, even the Amish and Mennonite children received a Christmas plate, although they were no longer told that these gifts came from the Christ Child. By that time, oranges and clear toy candy were added to the cookies and schnitz.

Cookies and Candy

By the mid-1800s, most Pennsylvania German families were making vast amounts of cookies, rolled and cut into fancy shapes with cutters made by the local tinsmith. Horses, cats, dogs, birds, and even elephants and camels were

common shapes. (Real elephants and camels might be seen on exhibit at the local tavern.) These cookies sometimes lasted into the new year, perhaps as late as February. In the cities, housewives competed for status by decorating and displaying iced cookies in their windows, each trying to outdo her neighbor.

Making candy was a double holiday treat. The work was turned into a social event, and taffy pulls were especially enjoyed by the teenagers. Candy makers boiled molasses, sugar, and water to the right consistency, allowed the mixture to cool, and then pulled it until it was white and creamy. Some people flavored the taffy with mint. The taffy, often sold in long strips, was called bellyguts, perhaps because of its resemblance to hog intestines.

Mooschi also was a favorite candy. It was just molasses, brown sugar, and butter cooked together, and then cooled in buttered tins with nuts sprinkled on top.

Christkindl and Belsnickel

Christmas celebrations were divided into two parts: religious and popular or secular. The Christ Child (Christkindl) was the main reli-gious figure. Belsnickel, a scruffy character dressed in rags and castoff clothing, led the secular festivals.

People believed that the Christ Child was the gift giver. Eventually, Christkindl became the word meaning the actual gifts instead of the giver. The Christ Child wasn't seen but was said to come through the keyhole.

Belsnickel, however, was seen and heard— and often feared. Belsnickel carried whips or switches, and he (or she) often used them to punish disobedient children. Most plain religious folks, including Amish and some Mennonites and Brethren, didn't believe in Belsnickel.

Belsnickel also gave food gifts. The proud and predominantly self-reliant people were often reluctant to accept charity. If Belsnickel gave gifts of food, however, the recipients couldn't refuse. In this way, our ancestors managed to help provide for needy widows and children. Belsnickel might provide a nice smoked ham, dried fruits, crocks of apple butter or sauerkraut, scrapple or pickled pig's feet, and basics such as bread, flour, lard, and butter.

Santa Claus became popular in the Pennsylvania German culture by the late 1800s.

"Father and I went to Lancaster to purchase the Market stall.
Bought the 2 for $10. Left Lancaster at 11.
Opened 200 oysters for our Christmas dinner."

PETER C. HILLER DIARY, DECEMBER 24, 1881

Roast Turkey and Sauerkraut

Following is a recipe for a traditional Christmas dinner of the 1800s. To roast in a modern oven, place turkey in a covered roasting pan and roast at 350 degrees for 4 to 5 hours for a 10- to 12-pound turkey.

Wash a nice young turkey and remove excess fat. Put turkey in a large Dutch oven and set on a bed of hot coals. Place hot coals on top of the lid. Be sure to place about 2 inches of water in the bottom of the Dutch oven. Roast about 2 hours.

Remove lid. Add about 2 quarts of sauerkraut in the bottom of the Dutch oven, along with about 2 cups water. Place back on the bed of coals, replace lid, and put fresh coals on top of lid. Roast another 4 hours, or until the turkey is soft and nicely browned. The amount of roasting time will depend on your wood and the size of the turkey.

The coals must be replaced quite often to keep the bird roasting well.

Shredding sauerkraut.

Mulled Cider

1 gallon apple cider
3 cinnamon sticks
1/2 cup brown sugar
10 whole cloves
8 whole allspices
dash of salt

Place all the spices in small cheesecloth bag and add to the cider in a large kettle. Add salt and sugar. Bring to a boil and simmer for an hour. Let sit for about 12 hours. Strain and reheat and serve warm.

Gumbis

1 small head of cabbage
butter
2 or 3 small tart apples
2 or 3 medium-size onions
1 cup leftover meat
    (optional)

This is a very old peasant dish consisting of layers of cabbage, onions, and apples. It can be flavored with leftover meats such as cooked ham, fried bacon, or sausage. It can be cooked slowly for several hours in a stewpot or in an oven casserole at 350 degrees for 1 to 1 1/2 hours, or you can use a modern electric crockpot.

Cut the cabbage in small pieces, and fry in a little butter just until slightly wilted. Peel onions, cut in thin slices, and set aside. Peel apples and cut into thin slices. Place ingredients in layers in a stewpot. Start with cabbage; then add onions, then cabbage, then apples. Continue to alternate, ending with cabbage. If you desire, meat can be added with each layer. Fill pot with water or meat broth and cover. If you don't have a lid, use a large cabbage leaf to cover. Place the stewpot on a trivet and surround it with hot embers. Start with just a shovelful of embers until the pot has warmed a little. Then pile lots of embers around pot and cook 2 hours or more.

Pennsylvania Germans usually chose a cedar tree for Christmas, or they cut wild cherry branches and fashioned them into a "tree," then decorated the branches.

Lacy Rolls or Cookies

1 cup sifted flour
1/2 cup shortening (butter)
1/2 cup molasses
1/8 teaspoon salt
1/3 cup granulated sugar
1 teaspoon ginger

Sift flour, ginger, salt, and sugar. Heat molasses to boiling point. Add shortening. Stir well. Add flour mixture slowly, stirring constantly. Drop by teaspoonfuls 3 to 4 inches apart on a greased tin. Bake at 350 degrees until golden brown, 8 to 10 minutes. Allow cookies to cool slightly before removing. You can roll the cookies up if wanted.

Grandmother's recipe (over 100 years old), contributed by Luella Hainley

"An 1871 Lancaster County farm Christmas dinner
included nuts, cakes, candies, turkey, sweet potatoes,
celery, sausage, faschtnachts (doughnuts),
custard, apple and mince pie."

ALFRED L. SHOEMAKER, 1959

Caramel Pudding

1 cup brown sugar
1 quart milk
1 egg
2 tablespoons cream
butter the size of a walnut
  (about 2 tablespoons)
2 heaping tablespoons
  cornstarch

Melt butter in a heavy kettle, and add the brown sugar and cream. Cook over high heat, stirring constantly, until very dark brown. It may take 5 to 8 minutes to get it brown enough. Dissolve the cornstarch in a little milk; then add with the egg to the rest of the milk. Beat well. Add the milk mixture to the caramel mixture. It will turn to a hard, taffylike mixture, but as the milk heats up, it will dissolve. Bring to a boil, and boil until thickened. Pour into a dish and serve cold. If desired, put a few chopped nuts on top before serving.

Coconut Snaps

2¹/₂ cups brown sugar

1 pint molasses
  (King Syrup)

3 cups flour

1¹/₂ cups finely grated
  coconut

2¹/₂ cups granulated sugar

¹/₄ pound butter

1 teaspoon baking soda

Heat molasses until warm, and add butter until it is melted. Mix the sugars together, and add the molasses-butter mixture. Stir in flour and baking soda. Add coconut. Refrigerate about 2 hours. Then roll small amounts of dough into small balls about the size of a large pea. These are best placed on a cookie sheet lined with parchment paper. Bake in a 350-degree oven for about 8 minutes. These cookies spread a lot and are very thin. They will bubble in the oven. As soon as the air bubbles fall, take them out of the oven, and the cookies will finish baking on the cookie sheet. Allow to cool before removing.

Salem Fancy Cakes

2 cups sugar
1 tablespoon lard
$^1/_2$ **nutmeg, grated**
$2^1/_2$ **to 3 cups flour**
$^1/_2$ **cup butter**
2 eggs
$^1/_4$ **teaspoon baking soda**

Cream butter, lard, and sugar. Beat in eggs. Add grated nutmeg. Blend in $2^1/_2$ cups flour and the baking soda. Add more flour if necessary, but don't make the dough too stiff. Refrigerate for about 2 hours. Roll out very thin and cut with cookie cutters. Place on cookie sheets, greased only the first time. Brush the cookies with egg wash (1 egg beaten with 1 tablespoon of water) before baking. Bake at 350 degrees for about 10 minutes, or until lightly browned. Makes approximately 100 medium-size cookies.

John Baer's Almanac, *1835, Lancaster, Pennsylvania*

Stormfitty Nut Cake (Plum Cake)

$1^1/_2$ **cups butter**
4 eggs, separated
1 teaspoon baking soda
1 cup raisins
1 small wine glass brandy
2 cups brown sugar
1 cup buttermilk
4 cups flour
1 cup chopped nuts

This recipe is really what was commonly called plum cake by the Pennsylvania Germans, and it was usually served as a Christmas treat. In the past, "plums" meant raisins.

Mix buttermilk and baking soda, and set aside. Cream butter and brown sugar. Beat in egg yolks. Blend in brandy. Now alternately add buttermilk and flour. Blend in stiffly beaten egg whites. Fold in raisins and nuts, and pour into a large greased and floured bundt pan. Bake at 350 degrees for at least 1 hour, or until done. Let sit for several hours and then serve.

Laura Henrietta (Hensel) Weaver, 1870–1900

"We had a very fat goose for Dinner."

HENRY H. LANDIS DIARY, DECEMBER 25, 1876

Apple Pie

6 to 8 tart apples
1¹/₂ tablespoons flour
1 tablespoon butter
pie dough for a double-
    crust 9-inch pie
³/₄ cup brown sugar
cinnamon to taste
rind and juice of ¹/₂ lemon
    (optional)

Peel and core apples, and slice into eighths. Mix with flour and brown sugar. Toss in lemon juice and rind if desired. Place the mixture into a pastry-lined 9-inch pie dish. Sprinkle with cinnamon and dot with butter. Place on a top crust. Pinch and seal crusts together, and trim off excess. Cut in steam vents. Bake in a 400-degree oven for about 1 hour.

Bellyguts (Pulled Taffy)

2 cups sugar
1 teaspoon cream of tartar
1 cup water
butter the size of a walnut
    (2 tablespoons)

Place all ingredients in a large kettle, and boil without stirring until a little dropped in cold water forms a hard crack. Place on a buttered platter and let sit until cool enough to handle. Then pull until taffy is smooth and nice and white. It can be flavored with spearmint or peppermint flavoring. Place a little flavoring on your hands and work it in. When it's nice and white, pull into long strips. Cut into bite-size pieces and wrap in small pieces of wax paper.

Mooschi or Moshey Pan Candy

1 cup brown sugar
1 tablespoon butter
1 tablespoon water
1 cup molasses (King
    Syrup)
1 teaspoon vinegar

Mix all ingredients together in a saucepan and boil until the mixture reaches a hard crack stage, meaning that a drop of the mixture becomes very hard and brittle when dropped in a cup of ice-cold water. Remove from the heat and add ¹/₂ cup of black walnuts if desired. Place in a buttered 8-inch square pan or several little buttered tart pans. Let get cold and then dump out of pans. Crack into small pieces to eat. This was a favorite Christmas candy.

Clear Toy Candy

2 cups granulated sugar

²/3 cup corn syrup or one
  small handful

¹/2 cup water

1 or 2 drops red or green
  food coloring
  (optional)

Oil clear toy molds with olive oil. Put the molds together and tie them shut tightly with string. (The modern-day method is to use heavy rubber bands.) Combine sugar, water, and corn syrup in a heavy 2-quart saucepan. Put over medium heat and stir until sugar is dissolved. Brush down the sides of the kettle with a brush to get rid of sugar crystals. Now boil without stirring until it reaches the hard crack stage (300 degrees). Add coloring if desired. (The natural color of the candy is yellow or amber.) It will mix in without stirring. Allow the mixture to stop boiling and pour into molds. Let cool. Remove strings or rubber bands, and pry open molds with a screwdriver. (Most molds actually have a slot for that purpose.) If too warm, the candy won't hold its shape. If too cold, it won't release.

Popcorn Balls

1 cup brown sugar

¹/2 cup heavy cream

1 cup whole peanuts

1 cup molasses
  (King Syrup)

4 quarts popped
  popcorn

Pop the popcorn and place in a large mixing bowl. Mix the sugar, molasses, and cream in a heavy kettle. Bring to a boil and cook, stirring constantly, until it reaches the soft ball stage, meaning a little of the mixture forms a firm but soft ball when dropped in a cup of ice-cold water. Take off the heat, stir in the peanuts, and pour over the popcorn. Mix well, using a large wooden spoon. Let the mixture sit for 5 to 10 minutes. Then butter your hands well and shape into balls, pressing them together rather tightly. Place on cookie sheets covered with buttered wax paper to cool. When cold, put in tight tins until ready to serve. Will keep several weeks.

Moravian Sugar Cake

1 cup mashed potatoes
1/4 pound butter
1 cup scalded milk
1 teaspoon salt
1 package yeast
2 eggs
1/2 cup granulated sugar
4 to 5 cups flour

Mix potatoes, milk, salt, sugar, butter, and milk. Let sit until luke-warm. Add eggs and yeast. Blend in enough of the flour to make a soft dough. Knead and place in a greased bowl. Let rise in a warm place for about 1 1/2 hours. Punch down and place in three greased 9-inch cake pans. Let rise; then punch full of holes. Fill the holes with butter and brown sugar, and sprinkle with cinnamon. Bake at 375 degrees for 15 to 20 minutes, or until nicely browned. Serve warm.

Moravian Dark Cakes

1/2 pound butter
1 tablespoon cream
1/2 teaspoon baking soda
scant 1/2 tablespoon ginger
1 teaspoon baking powder
1 cup sugar
2 cups dark molasses
   (New Orleans)
1 tablespoon cinnamon
1/2 teaspoon ground
   cloves
8 cups flour

Cream butter and sugar; then add cream and molasses. Blend together spices, baking powder, baking soda, and flour. Stir flour mixture into butter mixture; dough will be fairly stiff. Refrigerate overnight. Roll out very thin on a well-floured board. Cut into various shapes with cookie cutters. Place on lightly greased cookie sheets. Egg wash the cookies with 1 egg beaten with 1 tablespoon of water, and sprinkle with a little sugar if desired. Bake at 350 degrees for about 8 to 10 minutes.

Sand Tarts

1 1/4 pounds butter
5 eggs
1 small teaspoon cream
   of tartar
2 pounds granulated
   sugar
4 pounds flour

Cream butter and sugar and then the remaining ingredients. Mix all ingredients together. Flavor with brandy, rose water, or lemon. Roll thin. Cream butter and sugar and then add rest. Sprinkle with granulated sugar, cinnamon, and broken nuts. Bake at 350 degrees until lightly browned.

Grandmother Kate Roland 1900, contributed by George Roland

Sand Tarts

2 pounds granulated
   sugar
1 1/4 pounds butter
2 pounds flour
3 eggs

Mix sugar and butter together. Beat in eggs. Add sifted flour to the sugar and eggs. Roll out very thin, and cut out cookies with cookie cutters. Sprinkle with sugar or walnuts. Bake at 350 degrees until lightly browned.

Mother's recipe, contributed by Luella Hainley

Raisin-Filled Cookies

2 cups granulated sugar

1 cup milk

4 teaspoons cream of
tartar

2 teaspoons baking soda

7 cups all-purpose flour

1 cup lard

2 eggs

2 teaspoons vanilla

2 teaspoons baking
powder

raisin filling (see recipe
below)

Sift flour, baking soda, cream of tartar, and baking powder together and set aside. Cream sugar and lard; then add eggs and vanilla. Beat well. Add milk and flour alternately. Roll dough out thin, and cut with a glass or biscuit cutter. Place on lightly greased cookie sheet. Top each cookie with about $1/2$ teaspoon of raisin filling. Cut out another cookie, place on top of raisin filling, and press edges of cookies together to seal. To make a more attractive cookie, cut a hole in the center of the top cookie with a very small cutter before placing it on top of the filling. It makes a sort of open-faced cookie. Bake at 350 degrees until lightly browned. Do not bake too dark.

Raisin Filling

2 cups raisins

1 cup water

juice and rind of one
lemon

1 cup granulated sugar

2 teaspoons flour

Mix the sugar and flour together in a small saucepan. Gradually blend in water to make a smooth paste. Add lemon juice and raisins. Bring to a boil, boil for 2 minutes, and then take off the heat. Add the lemon rind and allow to cool thoroughly before using.

CHAPTER 10

New Year's Day
Shooting In the New Year

"The old custom of firing off the old year was duly honored this evening by a noisy congregation of men and boys."

JAMES L. MORRIS DIARY, DECEMBER 31, 1845

Don't take manure from the barn on New Year's Day or you'll take dead animals out all year long.

PENNSYLVANIA GERMAN FOLKLORE

For many years, Pennsylvania Dutchmen observed the New Year's holiday by shooting out the old year and shooting in the new one—literally.

After the chores were done on New Year's Eve, friends and family gathered to greet the New Year. Groups of young men known as firing parties or shooting parties traveled from house to house or farm to farm. At each place, they shot off the old year by firing their shotguns. They sent the residents of each house good wishes by singing or chanting special verses. Afterward, the men were invited into the houses for food and drink and brief social visits.

Then it was on to the next house to repeat the process. With some, it was a solemn occasion rather than a boisterous one. Members of the firing parties were a select, elite group who could not join without a special invitation from the senior members.

The meal on New Year's Day was always pork and sauerkraut, because the pig roots forward and would ensure success and good luck in the coming year.

Sauerkraut and pork is the traditional New Year's meal for any self-respecting Pennsylvania German.

Pork and sauerkraut.

Apple Pudding

3 apples, peeled and finely
    diced

1/2 teaspoon cinnamon

1/2 cup currants, fresh or
    dried

1/2 cup sugar

juice and rind of 1/2 lemon

1 1/2 cups freshly grated
    bread crumbs

4 tablespoons butter

1/4 cup sugar

3 eggs, separated

1 cup milk

Mix the first six ingredients together and set aside. Cream the butter with 1/4 cup sugar. Beat in the egg yolks and milk. Blend all ingredients together, then fold in the stiffly beaten egg whites. Place in a large redware baking dish, and sprinkle with nutmeg. Bake at 350 degrees for 40 to 45 minutes.

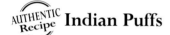 **Indian Puffs**

Bring 1 pint milk to a boil. Gradually add 4 tablespoons sugar and 4 tablespoons Indian meal [cornmeal]. Turn out into a bowl and let cool to lukewarm. Add 1/4 of a fresh grated nutmeg. Beat 4 eggs until light and add to the mixture. Bake in 4 greased custard cups. Cups will be about 3/4 full. Bake at 350 degrees for about 40 minutes. Serve warm like a bread or muffin.

Pennsylvania Farm Journal, *1855, Philadelphia*

Newmarket Pudding

Heat just to a boil 1 pint of milk with half a lemon peel and just a little cinnamon. Sweeten with a half cup of sugar. Beat 3 eggs in a basin, slowly add milk and beat well, discard lemon peel. Slice bread or rolls very thin and butter each piece. Place in a quart-sized baking bowl, alternating the bread with a layer of dried cherries. Pour the liquid over the bread and cherries and bake in a moderate oven about 1 hour. Cool slightly, unmold and serve warm.

The Cook's Oracle, *1823, Boston*

Red Cabbage with Apples

2 1/2 pounds red cabbage

1 teaspoon salt

1/2 cup vinegar

1/2 teaspoon allspice

3 large apples, peeled, cored, and sliced

2 slices salt pork

1/8 teaspoon pepper

1/4 teaspoon ground cloves

1/2 cup sugar

Dice salt pork and brown in Dutch oven. Remove and set aside. Slice cabbage and place in pot with pork fat. Add all other ingredients except apples and vinegar. Barely cover with water, cover Dutch oven, and bring to a boil. Lower heat and cook until almost tender. Add vinegar and continue cooking 10 to 15 minutes. Add apples. Cook about 5 minutes longer, until apples are soft but not mushy. Drain and serve hot. This is very good served with pork.

Baked Oysters

4 tablespoons butter
1 cup bread crumbs
1 pint small oysters
$^1/_4$ teaspoon salt
$^1/_8$ teaspoon paprika
$^1/_4$ teaspoon
    Worcestershire sauce
1 teaspoon chopped
    parsley
6 strips bacon

Melt butter. Mix together the butter, bread crumbs, salt, paprika, and parsley. Add the oysters and Worcestershire sauce and stir into the crumbs. Place this mixture in a shallow baking dish. Arrange the bacon over the top and bake 15 minutes in a moderate oven.

Grandmother's recipe, c. 1900, contributed by George Roland

Pork and Sauerkraut

3- or 4-pound pork roast
2 baking apples
2 quarts sauerkraut
$^1/_4$ cup brown sugar (more
    or less, depending on
    the tartness of the
    sauerkraut)
salt and pepper

Put pork into a large roasting pan, fat side up. Sear all sides of the meat on top of the stove. Arrange the sauerkraut on top and around the pork. Thinly slice the apples and mix with the sauerkraut. Add brown sugar and stir it well into the sauerkraut. Add enough water to nearly cover the sauerkraut. Bake at 450 degrees for 15 minutes. Reduce the heat to 375 degrees and bake until the meat comes off the bones when stuck with a fork. Serve with mashed potatoes.

Julia Lewis, c. 1930

Waffles

1 pint flour
$^1/_4$ pound butter
a pinch of salt
1 pint light cream
3 eggs, separated

Melt butter, and add cream and well-beaten egg yolks. Blend in flour and salt. Last, fold in stiffly beaten egg whites. Bake immediately in a hot greased waffle iron. Makes about 12 waffles. The waffle batter can be flavored with a little cinnamon, nutmeg, or rose water before baking.

Lemon Wafers

¹/4 cup butter
¹/2 nutmeg, grated
juice and rind of 1 lemon
¹/2 cup granulated sugar
3 eggs
flour to make stiff batter
   (approximately 1¹/2
   cups)

Cream butter and sugar. Beat eggs until light and add to butter and sugar mixture. Add lemon, nutmeg, and flour. Beat well until smooth. Bake immediately in hot wafer iron. (It must be a wafer iron, *not* a waffle iron. Wafers are thin and crispy like an ice cream cone. Wafer irons are available from a gourmet shops.) Note: Heat the iron in the fire until it is hot enough that it smokes when you open it. Grease the iron. Hold the open iron level on a table, and put 1¹/2 to 2 tablespoons batter directly in the center. Close up quickly and place back on the fire about 1 minute. Flip the iron and let it on the fire another minute. If a lot of batter comes out of the iron, use a little less batter. Also, cut excess batter off of the iron with the back of a knife before opening the iron. Wafers and waffles seem only to have been made for holidays, especially Christmas and New Year's.

Philadelphia Cookbook, *late 1800s*

Common Cup Cake

¹/2 cup butter
1 cup sugar
¹/2 teaspoon baking soda
juice and rind of 1 lemon
¹/2 cup buttermilk
3 eggs
¹/2 nutmeg, grated
2 cups all-purpose flour

Cream butter and sugar. Add eggs. Blend in the lemon juice and rind. Add buttermilk, flour, baking soda, and nutmeg. Bake in 6 greased and floured cups for about 30 minutes at 350 degrees.

Mrs. Koechling, 1850–90

AUTHENTIC Recipe **An Outstanding/Extraordinary Punch**

In the last war an English Admiral gave the officers in his fleet and other invited guests a punch. This used 600 flasks of cognac, 600 flasks of rum, 1200 bottles of Malag wine, 4 tons Pochenden waters, 600 pounds of sugar, 200 pieces grated nutmeg, and the juice of 2600 lemons. Instead of a punch bowl, serve in a basin of marble.

American City and County Calendar, *1799, Philadelphia*

"New Year Greeting good luck to all my Friends & Peace to my Enemies. I am not keeping this day as a Holiday. I and Jacob are Striping Tobacco."

HENRY H. LANDIS DIARY, JANUARY 1, 1889

Photo by Michael A. Occhionero

"Rose as usual about 6 a.m. there was very little New Year Shooting last night and only one shot this morning."

HENRY H. LANDIS DIARY, JANUARY 1, 1914

CHAPTER 11

Groundhog Day
The Grundsau Says . . .

*On February 2, the
farmer should have half
his hay and straw left.
To be a good housewife,
the woman should be done
with winter spinning.*

PENNSYLVANIA GERMAN
FOLKLORE

Long before the weatherman appeared on the six o'clock TV news, the Pennsylvania Dutch were foretelling the weather by observing and interpreting the natural signs in their world around them.

Perhaps the best known of these "forecasters" is the groundhog. Few people today are unfamiliar with the belief that if the groundhog sees his shadow on February 2, there will be six more weeks of winter.

But it was the Pennsylvania Dutch who created a Grundsau Lodsch (Groundhog Lodge) to spotlight the groundhog's talents, as well as to preserve and perpetuate the Pennsylvania German heritage through songs, speeches, stories, fellowship, and food. These lodges are still going strong—almost as strong as a Dutchman's appetite.

The Sleepy Cook from **The Comic Almanac.**
Landis Valley Museum Collection, PHMC

*"Roads very muddy
ankle deep in most places.
Had 100 oysters brought from
Lancaster. Price $1.00."*

PETER C. HILLER DIARY,
JANUARY 28, 1879

Griddle Cakes

3 slices stale bread
$^1/_4$ cup flour
$^1/_2$ teaspoon baking soda
1 cup boiling water
1 egg

Pour boiling water over the bread and stir until it forms a smooth paste. Add flour, egg, and baking soda. Drop by tablespoonfuls onto a hot griddle. Brown one side, then flip over and brown the other side. Serve with butter and syrup.

Cornmeal Griddle Cakes

4 tablespoons cornmeal
2 tablespoons butter
$^3/_4$ cup milk
$1^1/_2$ tablespoons flour
1 egg
dash of salt

Heat milk and butter until the butter melts. Stir in the cornmeal and flour. Add salt and egg. Beat well and fry immediately on a hot griddle. Fry until brown on one side; then flip over and brown the other side. Serve hot with butter and syrup.

Molasses Cup Cake

$^1/_2$ dark molasses
   (New Orleans)
1 egg
$^1/_2$ cup milk
$^1/_2$ teaspoon baking soda
$1^1/_2$ to 2 cups flour
$^1/_2$ cup granulated sugar
$^1/_2$ cup lard
spices to taste, such as
   $^1/_2$ teaspoon cinnamon,
   dash ground cloves,
   and nutmeg

Cream lard and sugar. Add the egg. Blend in the molasses and spices. Sift $1^1/_2$ cups flour with the baking soda. Add alternately with the milk. Add more flour if batter is too thin. Grease and flour 6 custard cups. Fill about $^1/_2$ full, and bake at 350 degrees for about 20 to 25 minutes.

Mrs. Koechling Cookbook, 1850–90

Mush

5 cups water
2 cups water
2 cups roasted cornmeal
1 tablespoon salt

Bring 5 cups of water and the salt to a rolling boil. Mix the corn-meal and 2 cups of water into a paste. When smooth, add to the boiling water, after taking it off the heat. The mush will lump up if added to the rapidly boiling water. Place back on the stove and cook slowly for about 45 minutes. Mush was made from Maine to Georgia during the eighteenth century; however, the Pennsylvania Germans were unique in that they roasted their corn before grinding. The first documented account of mush in Pennsylvania was from 1787 in Lancaster.

Mush Muffins

1 quart cooked mush
2 cups warm milk
1 tablespoon butter
10 to 12 cups flour
1 tablespoon salt
1 tablespoon sugar
1 teaspoon dry yeast

Add milk, butter, sugar, and salt to fresh cooked mush. Cool to lukewarm. Mix yeast with only about 2 cups of the flour. Beat this into the liquid, and then add enough flour to make a moderately stiff dough. Let rise overnight. Punch down and knead a few minutes. Roll out about 1 inch thick. Cut with a glass or biscuit cutter. Place on a floured board. Let rise until doubled. Fry on a hot, lightly greased griddle. Turn over and fry the other side.

Mammy Fry's Pie Dish Cake

2 cups brown sugar

1 cup lard

1 teaspoon cream of tartar

2 cups thick milk
(buttermilk)

1 tablespoon baking soda

flour to make stiff, about
4 cups

Add baking soda to the buttermilk and set aside. Cream the lard and brown sugar, add the buttermilk mixture, and stir in the cream of tartar and the flour. Divide the batter between 3 greased and floured pie dishes. Bake at 350 degrees for 20 to 25 minutes.

Mammy (Amanda) Fry, c. 1848–1920, contributed by Tom Martin

Schnitz un Knepp (Apples and Dumplings)

1 smoked ham butt, about
3 pounds

2 cups apple schnitz
(sliced, dried apples)

2 tablespoons brown sugar

cloves or ground
cinnamon to taste
(optional)

knepp (see recipe below)

Cover the schnitz with water and soak overnight. The next morning, put the ham in a heavy cooking pot and add cold water to cover. Bring to a boil, reduce heat, cover, and simmer over medium heat for 2 hours. (Precooked ham will take only about 30 minutes.) When tender, remove the ham and take it from the bone. Cut the meat into bite-size pieces and return it to the pan. Add the apples and the water in which they were soaked, as well as the brown sugar and spice, and cook 1 hour longer. Add the knepp (dumplings) the last 20 minutes.

Knepp

2 cups flour

1/2 teaspoon salt

2 tablespoons butter,
melted

1 tablespoon baking
powder

1 egg, beaten

scant 1/2 cup milk

Sift the dry ingredients into a large bowl. Stir in the beaten egg and melted butter. Add just enough milk to make a moderately stiff batter. Drop from a spoon into the boiling ham and apples. (If too much ham broth has evaporated, add 1 cup hot water to make enough liquid to cook the dumplings.) Cover the kettle tightly and simmer 20 minutes. Do not lift the lid during that time. Remove the dumplings with a slotted spoon and set aside, and pour the ham and apples onto a platter. Arrange the dumplings on top and serve at once.

Schpeck Supp (Soup)

1 pound bacon
5 finely chopped onions
1 quart milk
hunk of butter
pinch of baking soda
6 large potatoes
1 cup corn
1 cup tomato sauce
1 large tablespoon flour
salt and pepper to taste

Cut 1 pound bacon into cubes and fry until well browned. Drain and set aside, reserving the fat. Peel and dice potatoes and put them on to boil. Add the corn and cook until all is tender. Pour off any excess water from the potatoes and corn. Fry the onions in the bacon fat until lightly browned. Drain off excess fat. Add onions, bacon, butter, and flour to the potato-and-corn mixture. Add milk and bring almost to a boil; then add the tomato sauce with a pinch of soda. Add salt and pepper. Serves about 8.

 ## Mother Horst Bag Pudding

1 egg well beaten
2 tablespoons butter
1 scant teaspoon baking
   soda
2 teaspoons cream of
   tartar
3 tablespoons sugar
3/4 cup sweet milk
2 1/2 cups flour
a little salt

Mix well beaten egg and sugar together. Melt butter and add it and the milk to the egg and sugar mixture. Mix flour, cream of tartar, salt, and soda together and add to the other mixture. Place in a bag and tie the bag shut close to the mixture. Place into a kettle of boiling water. Place a lid on the kettle and boil 1 hour. Don't remove the cover until the pudding is boiled.

Frances (Sweigart) Horst, c. 1890, contributed by Clarke Hess

Photo by Michael A. Occhionero

Hog Maw (Pig's Stomach)

1 large pig stomach,
   cleaned

1 cup chopped onions

1 pound fresh bulk
   sausage

1/2 cup water

4 cups potatoes, diced
   small

2 tablespoons parsley

salt and pepper to taste

Mix together potatoes, onions, parsley, sausage, salt, and pepper. Loosely stuff mixture into the stomach. (Do not stuff too firmly or it will tear.) Put the stomach into a baking dish with the water. Bake, covered, at 350 degrees for 2 hours. Uncover and increase temperature to 400 degrees during the last 30 minutes.

CHAPTER 12

Funerals
Don't He Fit His Coffin Nice?

*Many small towns included people who attended funerals
even when they didn't know the deceased or the family.
They were the mitesser (the one who eats along) and
wunnerfitz (a curious or nosy person).*

Pennsylvania German Folklore

One of the greatest festive occasions among the Pennsylvania Germans was the funeral. Deaths weren't a reason for celebrating. Funerals, however, were an important time for socializing and eating, as well as remembering the dearly departed.

When a death occurred, friends of the family came to the house to take over chores and relieve the family of household and farm tasks. Also, friends would redd up (straighten up the house) and plan the food preparations for the funeral.

The news of the death was told by family and friends to additional family and friends by spreading the word or warning. In his diary, Henry H. Landis calls the people who carried the news of a death "warners."

Funeral Services

Depending upon the religious beliefs of the family and the time period, funeral services were held in the home, the meetinghouse (church), or both, and the sermons could be delivered in English or German. Until the 1870s, most funerals were held in the home.

Family members usually prepared the shroud and the body, which was laid out in the good Schtubb (parlor) for viewing. Before modern embalming techniques, the corpse was prepared in an eis box (ice box). As the ice melted, the dripping water marked a solemn death knell that was dreaded by the courting couples who often were chosen to sit up overnight with the corpse. In earlier times before ice was available, brandy-soaked rags were laid upon the body. Those who sat with the corpse had to change the cloths frequently.

The Laademacher (coffinmaker) was assigned the task of making the coffin. He built it to size to fit the corpse. Frequently heard at funerals was the compliment "Don't he fit his coffin nice?"

On the day of the funeral, people arrived early. Services could begin as early as eight-thirty or nine o'clock in the morning. Hostlers cared for the horses and marked them with chalk to

prevent mix-ups when visitors left for home at the end of the day.

Funeral Dinner

By eating the funeral dinner, the family took a major step in reuniting and restoring order to their lives. Food items were needed that would keep well and could be easily served.

Certain foods came to be associated with funerals because they were served so often on those occasions. For example, raisin pie became known as funeral pie. Dried foods and pickles were common fare before modern methods of preserving, so they frequently appeared at funeral meals.

Large crowds required making do. Sometimes tables were set up in a barn or wagon shed, and the guests ate in relays. Friends and neighbors served the food. The meals included cold meats, bread and butter, dried peaches, stewed prunes, pickles, and schmieres such as apple butter. Also, pies, rusks (rolls), cheese, and sometimes mashed potatoes and stewed chicken were served. Guests were almost always offered coffee, and sometimes wine was put upon the table.

Funeral Folklore

Much folklore relates to death and funerals. For instance, it was believed to be a sign of death if a bird entered the room through a window or down a chimney, if a horse neighed, if a dog barked at night, if a looking glass broke, if you dreamed about having a tooth pulled, or if you saw someone dressed in black.

No washing should be done when a corpse was in the house, according to old sayings. And it was disrespectful to walk across a grave; you should walk behind the headstone or past the foot of the grave.

It was believed that urinating into an open grave cured bed-wetting.

Supposedly, John Hall of Collegeville, Pennsylvania, was buried standing up so that he could look over his farm and watch what was happening.

To Make and Print Butter

butter churn
butter paddle
heavy whipping cream
ice
small wooden bowl
butter prints
salt (plain)
wide shallow bowl

"The bread we were raised on was the coarse rye bread—wheat bread or white bread being seen on the table only on special occasions like harvest, the holidays, or marriages and funerals. Hence the expression Weissbrot-Frolic (white bread frolic) as applied to funerals by thoughtless youngsters."

"A GRANDMOTHER'S MEMORIES," *THE PENNSYLVANIA-GERMAN,* 1907

Butter can be printed with a butter print or pushed into a butter mold, which may have a design carved into it. Scald the prints with boiling water, and then place them into a shallow bowl. Cover them with ice cubes, and fill the bowl with water. The prints need to stay submerged in the ice water. Meanwhile, rinse out your butter churn. The old rule of thumb was to rinse it with hot water in the winter and cold water in the summer. The cream should be at approximately 50 to 55 degrees; pour into the churn. The amount of cream is determined by the size of your churn, which should be between $1/3$ and $1/2$ full; do not overfill the churn. Put the lid on and start churning. If you are using the dasher type, just keep pulling it up and down; with a paddle churn, just turn the handle. Churning should be done at a steady, even pace, not too fast and not too slow. As you churn, you will feel the mixture getting stiffer, until it may feel almost impossible to churn. Once it reaches this stage, keep going until the mixture breaks. All of a sudden it will churn very easily, and that's when the globs of butter and the liquid separate. When this happen, keep going a little longer to get nice globs of butter.

It can take anywhere from 15 minutes to almost an hour to churn butter, depending on the weather and temperature. If it's extremely hot, the butter may not come; this sometimes can be corrected by adding a little ice to the cream. Now remove the lid and get the globs of butter out with your butter paddle, and place them in the wooden bowl. Just set the buttermilk aside. Next, work the butter from one side of the bowl to the other with your paddle, squeezing out the liquid. Pour this into a jar or bowl; this is just slop. Add ice water to the bowl, and again move the butter from one side of the bowl to the other. This is called washing the butter; you are trying to get rid of any excess buttermilk. Pour off the liquid and add more ice water. This needs to be done until the water runs clear. Then try to work the butter further to get rid of any water. It is now ready to salt; add about two pinches and work it in, and taste for saltiness. How much you use is a matter of personal taste. Salt adds flavor and helps preserve the butter a little longer.

Take your print or mold and press the butter into the wood. Press hard to get a good impression. The butter should level off with the bottom of the mold, and then it's ready to unfold. Pile the butter on top of the print about two inches deep. Use a table knife to smooth off the print and shape the butter like an upside-down ice cream cone. Now get a butter dish and press the butter on to the plate until it sticks. Don't press too hard. Wiggle the print a little bit, and the butter should release from the print. If it doesn't release, try to get the point of a sharp knife just under the edge of the butter, and this should get it to release. It takes a little practice, but you can get some really nice-looking butter. If you are making this butter for a party or dinner, you can do it several days or a week in advance. Place it in the freezer, and when frozen, wrap it in plastic wrap until ready to use.

To clean up the equipment, remove the buttermilk from the churn. You can either drink it or save it for future recipes. If the churn is glass or pottery, it can be washed with hot soapy water, rinsed, and dried. Wooden items should be washed with hot water and baking soda, as soap may impart a taste to the wood. Allow the churn, dasher, and paddle to dry thoroughly for about 24 hours before putting them back together again. Let all the wooden items air-dry well before putting them away.

Potato White Bread

3 or 4 medium potatoes

3 cups water

2 teaspoons salt

3/4 cup sugar

1 cup warm water

2 cups scalded milk

2 tablespoons shortening

2 tablespoons yeast

about 12 cups bread flour

Peel potatoes, cut up in small pieces, and boil in about 3 cups of water. When soft, drain potatoes, reserving 1 cup of the liquid. Mash potatoes or put them through a sieve. Then mix together the mashed potatoes, potato water, warm water, scalded milk, shortening, salt, and sugar. Add about 6 cups of flour to the mixture and beat well. Mix yeast with 2 cups of flour and add to the rest of the mixture. Be sure the mixture is lukewarm before adding yeast. Add enough more flour to make a moderately stiff dough. Knead well, until smooth and elastic. Place in a greased bowl, cover with a warm, damp cloth, and let rise for 2 hours. Knock down and shape into rolls or loaves of bread, approximately 5 loaves or 6 dozen rolls. Place in greased pans, cover with a cloth, and let rise for about 1 hour, or until doubled in bulk. Bake at 375 degrees about 20 minutes for rolls, or about 35 to 40 minutes for bread.

Gingerbread Cake

1 cup butter

2 cups granulated sugar

1/4 cup freshly grated
   ginger root

1 teaspoon baking soda

1 teaspoon cinnamon

3 eggs

1 cup dark molasses
   (New Orleans)

a dash of cloves

1 cup buttermilk

3 to 3 1/3 cups flour

Mix baking soda and buttermilk, and set aside. Cream butter and sugar, and add the eggs and molasses. Add the spices and freshly grated ginger root. Add the buttermilk and flour alternately. Pour into three 9-inch greased and floured baking pans. Bake at 350 degrees until done, approximately 30 to 35 minutes.

Some gingerbread with curd.

Spiced Cantaloupe

6 pounds cantaloupes
4 quarts water
1 quart apple cider
   vinegar
1 tablespoon whole cloves
1 tablespoon alum
3 pounds sugar
4 cinnamon sticks

Cut cantaloupes, remove seeds and rinds, and cut into bite-size pieces. Mix water and alum, and bring to a boil. Add the cantaloupe. Tie spices in a spice bag, and add to the water with the cantaloupe. Boil until the cantaloupe pieces look clear, about 20 minutes. Remove spice bag. Add vinegar and sugar to the cantaloupe mixture and bring to a boil. Place cantaloupe and liquid into hot glass canning jars, and seal with jar tops. *Note:* Cantaloupes should be rather firm ones, not too ripe, or they will become mushy when cooked.

 # Mennonite Communion Wine

For 1 gallon of wine take 2 quarts of Concord grapes that have benn washed and picked off the stems. Put into a gallon jug and add 3 pounds of sugar. Fill up the jug with water and allow to ferment 3 weeks at room temperature. Then strain and bottle, cork loosely as it will blow up the bottles if capped too tight. Should be ready to serve by Christmas. Place a small sand bag on top of the jug while fermenting to keep out the sour flies.

Lydia Zimmerman (Hoover) Martin, early 1900s,
contributed by Tom Martin

Sarah Snader Funeral Menu
Died May 27, 1914, Goodville, Pennsylvania

30 pounds of meat
10 loaves of bread at 7 cents a loaf
12 dozen buns
25 pounds of prunes

10 pounds of dried peaches
2 pounds of coffee
100 cigars
2 sticks of chalk

Raisin Pie (Funeral Pie)

1 pound raisins
3/4 cup brown sugar
4 cups water
2 tablespoons flour
2 eggs
juice and rind of 1 lemon

Soak raisins several hours or overnight. Then bring to a boil and add sugar and flour that have been blended together. Boil a few minutes and strain off some of the liquid. Beat the eggs well and slowly add some of the hot liquid to the eggs, continuing to beat as you add the liquid. Add all the liquid back into the raisins and bring again to a boil. Boil until thickened. Now add lemon juice and rind. Let cool thoroughly before putting into a pie shell. Put mixture in a 9-inch pie shell, place some dots of butter on top, and add a top crust. Bake at 400 degrees for about 45 minutes.

"[Paid] to Mrs. Boly to cash for laying out my mother and making the Shroud and for material for the Shroud."

HENRY H. LANDIS DAYBOOK, JUNE 18, 1881

Rusks (Rolls)

1 cup scalded milk
1 teaspoon salt
¹/₄ cup sugar
3 to 3¹/₂ cups flour
¹/₄ cup butter
2 eggs, well beaten
1 packet dry yeast

Scald milk; add butter, sugar, and salt. Let sit until lukewarm. Add eggs and yeast. Mix in just enough flour to make a relatively soft dough. Knead well and place in a greased bowl to rise. Punch down and shape into rolls, approximately 18 to 24, depending on size. Place in greased pans. Let rise until doubled in size. Bake at 375 degrees for about 20 minutes, or until nicely browned.

Jumbles

3 eggs
1 cup butter
1 teaspoon cinnamon
2 cups or more flour
2 cups sugar
1 tablespoon brandy
1 whole nutmeg, grated
juice and rind of 1 lemon

Cream sugar and butter. Beat eggs very light and add to the flour. Then add butter mixture to the flour mixture. Add spices, brandy, and lemon juice and rind. It may be necessary to add a little more flour. Take about 1 tablespoon of dough and roll out on a board with your hands into a long rope. Then curl up the rope into a snail-like little cookie. Place cookies on a lightly greased baking sheet. Place them close together, as they do not rise or spread very much. Bake in a 350-degree oven for about 10 minutes, or until the bottoms are lightly browned. They don't brown a great deal. *Note:* Be careful not to add too much flour to the dough, or the cookies will taste floury. However, 2 cups is generally not enough flour; it may take ¹/₂ to ³/₄ cup more. Serve as an afternoon cookie with wine.

CHAPTER 13

Vendues, or Public Sales
Going Once, Going Twice . . . Sold!!

A public sale, c. 1900.
Landis Valley Museum Collection, PHMC

"To a small boy, the most important part of the public sale were the huckster tables. These were tables about ten feet long covered with boxes of candy, peanuts, sometimes oranges, sometimes with the aid of a small oil stove oysters were stewed."

BIRDES JACOBS, 1952

The vendue, or public sale, has always been a big social event in the Pennsylvania German community. It represents both a beginning and an end. Whether it is a horse and cattle auction or the ever-popular farm sale, family and friends turn out in great numbers.

The farm sale, often including the content of house and barn, invokes a mixed bag of emotions. Many come seeking a bargain or a specific item that they need or want. Some come hoping to buy an aadenke (remembrance) of a dear friend or family member. Others come just to visit old friends or make new ones. And some come just for the free entertainment.

In the past, whole families attended sales "chust because it wondered them so." They were curious, and the sale fascinated them with all of its many aspects.

Often the farm sale marked an end of an era or a way of life. Sometimes it meant the death of a person or the end of a dream.

Grandpa's old plow or fishing pole might be for sale. Little sister's high chair or Aunt Fanny's rocking chair was sold to the highest bidder. Even Uncle Hutz's three-legged milking stool used when he milked Bessie the cow was put on the auction block.

The cattle auctions attracted scores of men. They could speculate about prices, argue the merits of one breed over another, and brag about animals long dead or still alive and kicking. As they talked, the stories took on lives of their own as one-upmanship prevailed. Each teller had to top the previous one as the biggest, the fastest, the hardest working, and the best trained were remembered. Which hogs had the biggest litters or gave the most lard when butchered vied with who had the orneriest mule—or at least claimed to have had.

Sometimes there was more action in the stories than there was on the sales platform. After all, this was before television, radio, and movies. People made their own entertainment.

Since vendues lasted a long time, food had to be provided in one way or another. In the 1800s, peddlers set up tables and sold such things as oyster stew, cakes, pies, candies, peanuts, and pretzels. Eventually, churches and other community groups entered the scene, providing chicken corn or ham and bean soup, as well as cakes and pies. Profits provided operating funds for their groups.

Today in Lancaster County, Pennsylvania, and surrounding areas, the farm sales still are a spring ritual. Many are sponsored by fire companies and similar organizations, and the profits continue to fund their activities.

Tobacco sales also are part of the area's history.

Landis Valley House Hotel and Sales Barn

In the late 1800s, a cattle auction barn, scales, hotel, and nearby blacksmith shop existed at Landis Valley. The Landis Valley House Hotel and sales barn next door provided a social meeting place to conduct business, tell tall tales, and argue politics.

The patrons may have settled their bills while munching on the hotel's famous ham sandwiches. They also enjoyed oxtail and snapper (turtle) soups. Because the main road from Lancaster to Reading went through Landis Valley, and the post office was located in the hotel, stagecoaches stopped there regularly. There were many reasons to visit the valley.

The father of the museum's founders, Henry Harrison Landis, often frequented the hotel. He met friends there, bought at the auctions, and imbibed an occasional drink at the hotel bar. His daily diaries and account books often mention these trips.

Leb Cookies

3 pounds light brown
  sugar
1 quart buttermilk
1 tablespoon vinegar
4 pounds flour
3/4 pound butter and
  Crisco
2 tablespoons baking soda
1 teaspoon salt
2 eggs

In a large bowl, combine sugar and shortening. Mix. Add 1 beaten egg. Dissolve baking soda in vinegar, and add to buttermilk. Alternately add flour and buttermilk to other ingredients, and mix. Put into refrigerator overnight. Next day, roll out dough about 1/4 inch thick and cut with cookie cutters. Place on greased cookie sheets and brush with second beaten egg. Bake at 400 degrees until lightly browned.

Grandmother's recipe, 100 years old, contributed by Louella Hainley

Mead or Sommer Bier (Summer Beer)

1 pint honey
1 teaspoon whole cloves
3 sticks cinnamon
1 quart water
4 cups granulated sugar
2 teaspoons yeast
3 quarts water

Mix first four ingredients together, bring to a boil, and simmer for 20 minutes. Strain out the spices and cool until lukewarm. Then add remaining ingredients. Mix all together and place in a gallon jug with a fermentation lock. Let ferment for about 3 weeks. Strain and place in a gallon jug, and lightly cork. (The mead may blow off the cork if fermentation is not complete. That's why the cork should not be tight.) The mead is ready to drink when it is clear, after 6 months or more. Pennsylvania Germans always spiced their mead and traditionally made it one summer to serve the following summer. They called it sommer bier (summer beer).

Crackers

1 quart flour
$^1/_2$ teaspoon salt
$^3/_4$ to 1 cup milk
2 ounces butter
1 teaspoon baking
    soda dissolved in
    2 tablespoons water

Mix the flour and salt, and cut in the butter. Add dissolved baking soda. Mix in enough milk to make it the consistency of pie dough. Beat with a wooden mallet for $^1/_2$ hour, turning and folding the dough. Roll out thin, cut with a biscuit cutter, and prick the tops. Bake at 350 degrees until lightly browned. Let in the oven until thoroughly dried.

John Baer's Almanac, *1850, Lancaster, Pennsylvania*

Snapper Soup

$3^1/_2$ **pounds veal knuckles**
$3^1/_2$ **quarts beef broth**
1 cup flour
1 cup chicken fat or butter
2 cups sherry
meat from 1 snapping
    turtle, ground into
    small pieces
3 onions, chopped fine
2 stalks celery, chopped
    fine
$^1/_4$ **teaspoon thyme**
1 bay leaf
3 lemon slices
salt and pepper
2 carrots, diced
2 cups tomatoes, strained
    through sieve
$^1/_2$ **teaspoon marjoram**
3 whole cloves
dash of Tabasco
1 hard-cooked egg,
    chopped

Veal knuckles should be broken into 2-inch pieces. Place knuckles in a roasting pan and add the butter or chicken fat, onions, celery, carrots, thyme, marjoram, cloves, bay leaf, and salt and pepper. Bake in 400-degree oven until brown. Remove from oven and gradually add flour, mixing well. Bake 30 minutes longer. Turn browned mixture into large kettle. Add the beef broth and tomatoes. Cook slowly for 3 to 4 hours. In a separate pan, combine the snapper meat with 1 cup of the sherry, salt, Tabasco, and lemon slices. Simmer for 10 minutes. Strain the soup and add the snapper mixture. Stir in the chopped egg and the remaining sherry. Serve immediately.

Abe's Snapper Soup

1 cup meat from 2 legs
    or the neck and tail
    of a snapping turtle

1¾ cups diced carrots

1 medium onion, chopped

2 cups milk, divided

2 heaping tablespoons
    flour

water

2 cups chopped celery

4 cups diced potatoes

1 tablespoon butter

salt to taste

First catch a turtle.

If you see a snapper while you're driving along, grab him by the tail and flip him into the back of your truck. When you're ready to clean him, flip him upside down. When his neck comes out to turn himself over, whack off his head. Snapper is the only turtle you can eat. The others are protected by law.

Cut around the neck and all around the shell to loosen the turtle from the shell. It's attached at the neck and the tail and has skin around the sides. Cut the breastplate off. Cut off the neck and legs. Separate the parts. Scald all the meat so the skin, toenails, and the tail bumps pull off easier.

Now you have the clean meat left. The legs are darker meat and can be used, but they are slightly stronger. The best parts are the white meat in the tail and neck.

Then give it to your wife to cook. (If you aren't married, you can't make Abe's snapper soup.)

Put turtle meat in kettle and cover with lightly salted water. (Use no more than 1 cup of turtle meat.) Cook until soft. It can take up to 3 hours, depending upon the age of the turtle. These are tough critters. After cooking, lay the meat aside to drain. Then bone and dice the meat. Discard the broth. Put carrots, celery, onion, and potatoes in kettle and cover with water. Add salt to taste. Cook until soft. Add 1 cup of the milk and butter. Mix the second cup of milk with the flour to make a white sauce, and add to the pot to thicken. Add the diced snapper meat. Heat through and serve. Do not boil.

Abe and Barbara Rissler

Crowds gather at the barn sale at Landis Valley, c. 1900. Landis Valley Museum Collection, PHMC

Cooked Salad Dressing

2 eggs
¹/₂ cup vinegar
¹/₂ cup water
¹/₂ teaspoon salt
¹/₄ teaspoon paprika
1 cup granulated sugar
2 tablespoons flour
butter the size of an egg
    (3 to 4 tablespoons)
pinch of pepper
1 tablespoon celery seed

In a kettle, melt butter and stir in flour. Beat eggs until lemon colored, and then add sugar, vinegar, and water. Add this to the butter-flour mixture, and cook until thickened. Stir constantly. Remove from heat and add salt, pepper, paprika, and celery seed. Let cool and pour over potato salad or use as a dressing for cabbage slaw.

CHAPTER 14

Medicines, Misfits, and Miscellaneous
Verhext and Verhuddelt

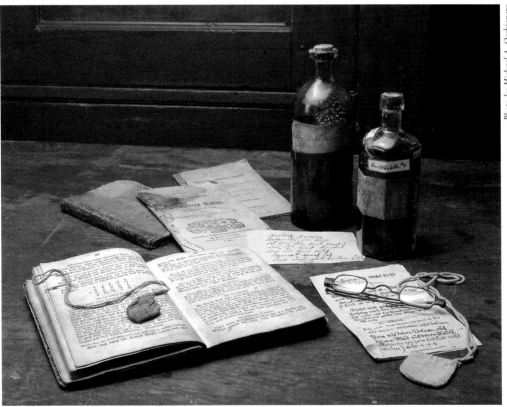

Photo by Michael A. Occhionero

*"This afternoon I met with an accident in the quarry I am
unable to [do] any work Just now Hen rubbed my back with
vinegar & salt it feels a little better now."*

Henry H. Landis Diary, January 7, 1876

This chapter is truly verhuddelt (confused). It contains all those miscellaneous bits of information too good to leave out.

The early German immigrants to this area of Pennsylvania believed in two main life forces: Hexerei and Braucherei. Hexerei (witchcraft) was the devil's work, and our ancestors did all they could to avoid being verhext (bewitched). Some wore an asafetida bag around their neck. Asafetida is a gum resin from an Asiatic plant and is known as Deiwelsdreck (devil's dirt) in the Pennsylvania Dutch dialect. It smells something like dirty old gym socks overlaid with garlic. Our ancestors must have believed that anything that smelled that bad must be powerful enough to keep the witches away.

To keep the evil spirits from entering structures, the Pennsylvania Dutch often place Himmelsbriefs (sacred notes from heaven) above the doors and windows of their houses and barns.

If, despite all their precautions, they still became ill or had a string of bad luck, they believed that they had been verhext and needed a good Braucher to break the spell. Braucherei, the opposite of Hexerei, means "to try for" and is a type of Pennsylvania German Christian faith healing based upon the Holy Bible.

In John George Hohman's *Long Lost Friend,* published in the early 1800s and reprinted in the 1900s, many guidelines were set forth to provide a healthy, happy life. For example, Hohman suggests this preventative treatment for hysteria and colds: "Every

*Pennsylvania Germans were familiar with powwow books,
asafetida bags, and balsam apples in bottles of whiskey.
They were some of the "cures" used in the 1700s and 1800s.*

evening pull off your shoes and stockings, run your fingers between all your toes and smell it. This will certainly effect a cure."

Hohman supports the idea that three is a holy number, as indicated in this remedy to stop bleeding: "This is the day on which the injury happened. 'Blood, thou must stop, until the Virgin Mary brings forth another son.' Repeat these words three times."

To make your chickens lay more eggs, Hohman says, "Take the dung of rabbits, pound it to powder, mix it with bran, wet the mixture till it forms lumps, and feed your chickens with it, and they will keep on laying a great many eggs."

From an unpublished manuscript written by Mary (Musselman) Stoner around 1862 to 1865 comes this method to stop bleeding—or, as Mrs. Stoner of West Earl Township in Lancaster County put it, "For to still Blut": "Steel a dish rack and ty the wons shut that shall be a very good sure." (If you don't read with a Pennsylvania Dutch accent, that means "Steal a dishrag and tie the wound shut. That shall be a very good cure.")

—✺—

"Frank was here this morning to pow wow [Braucherei] for my wild fire, [the painful skin disease erysipelas] which is very bad. My face looks as red as a turkey head."

HENRY H. LANDIS DIARY, JANUARY 10, 1889

 # Recipes

The Landis Valley Cookbook Committee strongly urges you *not* to try any of the recipes in this chapter. We include them only for their historical value and your enlightenment. All recipes in this chapter are authentic recipes in their original form.

This shall be a cure for the small Pox

"As soon that you know that it shall be the or come to the small pox to keep them bag so as they don't get so bad on you take as follows one half pint good sweat cream the yolk of 4 eggs beat well and white sugar so much for to make it rite good and sweet take this all as soon as you can if it makes you a little tipsey it do not hirt you enny."

A Cure for Consomson

"Take one quart of rupt horse redish 2 quarts of the best yellow vine in a new stone juck then berit in the cround 12 ourers than take it out and take one taple spoon for too mornig and then one teespone evere mornig."

For a Woman Before she is Going to her Child Bet

"Take one pint of licer and put som wachhulter ruts and som oland ruts in that licer as much as you sink that strong enuf take one spoonful 2 times a day for 4 weeks of it M.L."

Fer the wors or som prick

"When you come throw the wolds and see son bons of somsing det take the lower sight and rup the warzen or the prick and lay him just as he had lait before and go home."

Cure for Cold Fever

"Take prenasel flowers 3 to 5 or 7 to 9 and stir them in raw egg and stir it together and trink it down with flowers and all."

Anogher Cure for the Cramph

"Take one teesponeful of sweet out of a mans hat and make tee 1/2 cupful of tee."

Cow Cure

"A cure for cows when a cow has work hir calf back from hir take low worm water and wash the back right clin and crece it with work lard and put it to her and then give hir shel crout to eat that schawl keepe hir frown working it of, I cand tel the English name of the shel crout it croce in gardlings or out sight the fens and give little yellow flowers this cure old Matie Meyer she tolt us he was a old Dutchman in 1864."

Mushel Powder (for burns)

"Cure for burnd when the skin is of the burnd take mushel shells oud of the crick and put them in the fier and burn them right whel and make powder of them right fine and then spred the powder on the burnd part of the boddy."

All of the above from Mary (Musselman) Stoner, c. 1862–65

Cough Syrup

Put one quart hoarhound [mint] to one quart water and boil it down to a pint. Add two or three Stickes of licorice and A tablespoon of Essence of lemon take a tablespoon of the syrup three times A day or as often as the cough may be troublesome.

Jonathan Mast Ledger, 1863, contributed by Mim Stoltzfus

Cure for a Horses Eye

"Cut a peas of new linen of the sise of a quarter dollar threw wich pass a nedel with a strong thred in such a manner that you can drew it shut then put three live spiders taken from three corners of the hous drew it shut make three nots in it after which tie in the horses forehed so that it hangs just about the eye and leave it thear till it falls off of itself."

Henry Stoner, c. 1825

Uncle John's Receipt Number 87

"Parsley seed soaked in Whiskey for 24 hours, then sowed in a composition of 2 parts wood ashes 1 part earth and sprinkled with rainwater will sprout and grow in 15 minutes. So says the directions in Dr. Daniel Schmidt's German family medicine book of 1829."

Uncle John's Receipt Number 90

"Effectual remedy for a young ladies sore throat. Enclose it closely, yet tenderly with a man's shirt sleeve, and be sure you have an arm in it."

Both from Laura Henrietta (Hensel) Weaver, c. 1870–1900

To Make Ley [Lye Soap]

Warning: Dripping lye is *poisonous and dangerous!* Lye can destroy your skin and blind you if it gets into your eyes. Use *extreme caution* if you decide to try this recipe.

"Provide a large ash-tub, small at bottom and large at top. Set it on a form, so high that a large tub may stand under it. Make a hole, an inch in diameter, on one side, at the bottom of the tub. Lay bricks within this tub, about the hole, and put straw over them. To seven bushels of ashes, put three pailfuls of boiling water, two gallons of slacked lime, and one gallon of unslacked lime. Put the lime into the water, and let it stand some time, and then pour it in. After this, add one pailful of cold soft water, once an hour, for ten hours. Set a large tub under the ash-tub, to catch the drippings, and try the strength by an egg. If this rises so as to show a circle of the size of a ten-cent piece, the ley is right. If the egg rises higher, the ley must be weakened with water; if it does not rise so high, the ley is too weak, and there is no remedy but to go over the whole process. Much depends on the kind of ashes. Hickory ashes make the strongest ley; and one fourth less of this kind is needed, than of most other kinds."

Catherine E. Beecher published these instructions to make lye in 1841 in Boston in *A Treatise on Domestic Economy.* Source Book Press reprinted them in 1970. Beecher was *not* Pennsylvania German. However, this is the same way that our ancestors dripped lye, and these instructions are some of the best and clearest we have seen.

Later, caustic soda and store-bought lye replaced the dripped ash lye, as seen in the next recipe from a Pennsylvania German source.

To Boil Hard Soap

"Take 5 lbs. of white caustic Soda, and then take 5 gallons Soft water. When it comes to a boil, then add 20 lbs. of fat, then boil 2 hours, when done put 1 quart and 1 pinch of salt to 1 Kettle if fat is not salty, if salty not quite so much, about 1 quart may do."

Sallie E. Kupp, 1887

Receipt to Use Potatoes as a Substitute for Soap

Take as many potatoes as may be necessary at one Time, wash them clean & boil them, drain the Water from & mash them; after which mix them with fresh boiling water to the Consistency of Gruel, in which immerse the dirty clothes, & let them remain covered with the Mixture for 24 hours; then rub the Cloates out of it, & rince them thoroughly in cold water, & dry them, when they will be completely cleaned.

Potatoes used as above directed, entirely remove Grease & every Kind of Dirt from white or coloured Linnens or Cotton Clothes & in preparing Thread Linnen or Yarn for the Weaver, they supercede the Necessity of using Soap or Pot-Ashes or of boiling the Yarn of which every Person may be satisfied, who will take the Trouble of trying the Experiment—The Gruel can be given to the hogs after it is used.

Sarah Yeates Cookbook, 1767–1829, taken from Relp's Philad'a Gazette *of February 17, 1816*

Bibliography

Books

Boyertown Area Cookery. Boyertown, PA: Boyertown Area Historical Society, 1978.

Brown, John Hull. *Early American Beverages.* New York: Galahad Books, 1968

Der Deutschen Hausfrau Kochbuch Oekenoemische Recepte. Chicago: 1894.

Eshelman, Pauline Benedict. *The Diaries of Peter C. Hiller.* Elverson, PA: Olde Springfield Shoppe, 1994

Fegley, H. Winslow. *Farming Always Farming: A Photographic Essay of Rural Pennsylvania Land and Life.* Birdsboro, PA: Pennsylvania German Society, 1987

Gibbons, Phebe Earle. *Pennsylvania Dutch and Other Essays.* Philadelphia: J. B. Lippincott & Co., 1872; reprint, Mechanicsburg, PA: Stackpole Books, 2001.

Gilbert, Russell W. *Bilder un Gedanke: A Book of Pennsylvania German Verse.* Breinigsville, PA: Pennsylvania German Society, 1975

Groff, Betty. *Betty Groff's Pennsylvania Dutch Cookbook.* New York: A. S. Barnes & Company, 1973.

Haag, Earl C. *En Pennsylvaanisch Deitsch Yaahr.* Schuykill Haven, PA: *Call* Newspaper, 1990.

Heller, Edna Eby. *The Art of Pennsylvania Dutch Cooking.* New York: Galahad Books, 1968.

Hutchinson, Ruth. *The Pennsylvania Dutch Cook Book.* New York: Harper & Brothers, 1948.

Johnson, Elizabeth, *Landis Valley Museum: Pennsylvania Trail of History Guide.* Mechanicsburg, PA: Stackpole Books, 2002.

Kraybill, Donald B. *The Amish of Lancaster County.* Mechanicsburg, PA: Stackpole Books, 2008.

Leslie, Eliza. *Directions for Cookery, Being a System of the Art in Its Various Branches.* Philadelphia: E. L. Carey & A. Hart, 1837.

Lestz, Gerald S. *The Pennsylvania Dutch Cookbook.* New York: Grosset & Dunlap, 1970.

Lichten, Frances. *Folk Art of Rural Pennsylvania.* New York: Charles Scribners & Sons, 1946.

Long, Amos. *The Pennsylvania German Family Farm.* Brunigsville, PA: Pennsylvania German Society, 1972.

Marquart, John. *600 Miscellaneous Valuable Receipts Worth Their Weight in Gold.* Philadelphia: John E. Patter and Company, 1867.

Shoemaker, Alfred L. *Christmas in Pennsylvania: A Folk-Cultural Study.* Kutztown, PA: Pennsylvania Folklife Society, 1959; 40th anniversary ed., Mechanicsburg, PA: Stackpole Books, 1999.

———. *Eastertide in Pennsylvania: A Folk-Cultural Study.* Kutztown, PA: Pennsylvania Folklife Society, 1960; 40th anniversary ed., Mechanicsburg, PA: Stackpole Books, 2000.

————. *Traditional Rhymes and Jingles of the Pennsylvania Dutch.* Lancaster, PA: Intelligencer Printing Company, 1951.

Showalter, Mary Emma. *Mennonite Community Cookbook.* Scottsdale, PA: Herald Press, 1950.

Stine, Eugene S. *Pennsylvania German Dictionary.* Birdsboro, PA: Pennsylvania German Society, 1996.

Stoudt, John Joseph. *Sunbonnets and Shoofly Pies.* New York: A. S. Barnes & Company, 1973.

The Thomas R. Brendle Collection of Pennsylvania German Folklore. Vol. I. Lancaster, PA: Historic Schaefferstown, 1995.

Weaver, William Woys. *The Christmas Cook.* New York: Harper Collins, 1990.

————. *Country Scrapple: An American Tradition.* Mechanicsburg, PA: Stackpole Books, 2003.

————. *Pennsylvania Dutch Country Cooking.* New York: Abbeville, 1993.

————. *Sauerkraut Yankees: Pennsylvania Dutch Food and Food Ways.* Philadelphia: University of Pennsylvania Press, 1983; 2nd. ed., Mechanicsburg, PA: Stackpole Books, 2002.

Wilson, Jose. *American Cooking: The Eastern Heartland.* New York: Time-Life Books, 1971.

Yoder, Don. *Discovering American Folklife: Essays on Folk Culture and the Pennsylvania Dutch.* Mechanicsburg, PA: Stackpole Books, 2001.

————. *Groundhog Day.* Mechanicsburg, PA: Stackpole Books, 2003.

Yoder, Don, and Thomas E. Graves. *Hex Signs: Pennsylvania Dutch Barn Symbols and Their Meaning.* Mechanicsburg, PA: Stackpole Books, 2000.

Newspapers, Magazines, Booklets, and Almanacs

"About the Landis Brothers." *American-German Review.* Philadelphia: Carl Schurz Memorial Foundation, April 1941.

Agricultural Almanac for the Year 1829–54. Lancaster, PA: John Baer, 1829–54.

Agricultural Almanac for the Year 1855–59. Lancaster, PA: John Baer & Sons, 1855–59.

Agricultural Almanac for the Year 1860–71. Lancaster, PA: John Baer's Sons, 1860–71.

Americanischer Stadt and Land Calendar. Philadelphia, 1799.

Balmer, Daniel. *A Collection of New Receipts and Improved Cures for Man and Beast.* Near Chambersburg, PA, 1826.

Columbian Almanac. Philadelphia: Joseph McDowell, 1856.

Cottage Garden Almanac. Philadelphia: King and Baird, 1865, 1873.

Daily Evening Express. Lancaster, PA, 1857.

Farmer's Almanac and Housekeeper's Receipt Book. Philadelphia: John H. Simon, 1852.

Farmers' and Citizens' Almanac. Philadelphia, 1839.

Farmers & Mechanics Almanak. Philadelphia: Mentz and Rovoudt, 1843, 1847, 1848.

Fisher's Improved Housekeeper's Almanac, Philadelphia: Fisher and Brother, 1865.

"Folklore from the Diary of James L. Morris, 1845–1846." *Pennsylvania Dutchman.* Lancaster, PA: Intelligencer Printing Co., February 1952.

Glatfelter, Charles H. "The Pennsylvania Germans, A Brief Account of Their Influence on Pennsylvania." *Pennsylvania History Studies,* no. 20. University Park, PA: Pennsylvania Historical Association, 1990.

Heller, Edna Eby. "Receipt Books Old and New." *Pennsylvania Folklife* (Fall 1960), Lancaster, PA.

Housekeeper's Almanac. Philadelphia: Behm and Gerhart, 1886.

Jacobs, Birdes A. "Anecdotes from 'Barleen' —East Berlin, Adams County, Pennsylvania." *Der Reggeboge.* 24. Birdsboro, PA: *Journal of the Pennsylvania German Society,* 1990.

Keyser, Alan G. "Gardens and Gardening among the Pennsylvania Germans." *Pennsylvania Folklife* (Fall 1960), Lancaster, PA.

Kite's Town and Country Almanac. Philadelphia: Benjamin & Thomas Kite, 1817.

Lancaster Examiner. Lancaster, PA, 1863.

Lancaster Examiner & Herald. Lancaster, PA, 1858.

Lancaster Holiday Journal. Lancaster City, PA, 1868.

Lancaster Journal. Lancaster, PA, 1815.

Landis, Henry K. "Early Kitchens." *Pennsylvania German Society.* Norristown, PA: Pennsylvania German Society, 1939.

Moravian Cookbook of Tried Recipes. Lancaster, PA: Home Moravian Mission Society of the Moravian Church, 1905.

Moyer, Earl H., and Kay Moyer Krick. *Almanac Lore of the Pennsylvania Dutch.* Collegeville, PA: Institute on Pennsylvania Dutch Studies, 1975.

Pennsylvania Farm Journal. Lancaster, PA, 1851.

Pennsylvania Farm Journal. Philadelphia, 1855.

Pennsylvania Farm Journal. West Chester, PA, 1853.

Pennsylvania Packet and Daily Advertiser. Philadelphia, 1790.

Reppert, Bertha. *Herbs of the Zodiac.* Mechanicsburg, PA: Rosemary House, 1984.

Saturday Evening Post. Philadelphia, 1868.

Sauter, S. F. *The Hour Has Arrived.* Germany, 1845; reprint, Max Kade, State College, PA: German-American Research Institute, PSU, 1994.

Turner's Improved Housekeeper's Almanac and Family Receipt Book. Lancaster, PA, 1847.

Uncle Sam's Almanac. Philadelphia: Leary & Getz, 1856.

Village Record & General Advertiser. West Chester, PA, 1832.

Weaver, William Woys. "Swiss Foods and Foodways in Early Pennsylvania." *Swiss-American Historical Society Newsletter* 16, no. 2 (1980).

York County Almanac. York, PA: Hiram Young, 1877.

Zahm, Matthias. *The Lancaster County Historical Society.* Lancaster, PA: Lancaster County Historical Society, 1943.

Diaries, Ledgers, and Account Books

Brown, Jacob M. Manuscript Cookbook. Mount Joy, PA. Private Collection.

Koechling Family Manuscript Cookbook. Lancaster City, PA. Private Collection, 1850–90.

Landis, Henry H. Landis Valley, Lancaster County, PA, 1876–1924. Landis Valley Museum, Philadelphia Historical and Museum Commission.

Reist, Christian B. Rapho Township, Lancaster County, PA, 1855. Private Collection.

Stoner, Mary (Musselman). West Earl Township, Lancaster County, PA, 1862–65. Private Collection.

Weaver, Laura Henrietta (Hensel). Manuscript Cookbook. Strasburg, PA. Private Collection.

Yeates, Sarah. Manuscript Cookbook. Lancaster, PA, 1767–1829. Translated by Marian Brubaker, 1990. Landis Valley Museum Collection, Pennsylvania Historical and Museum Commission.

Index